THE ENGLISH BAPTISTS

OF THE

EIGHTEENTH CENTURY

A History of the English Baptists

Volume 2

General Editor: B. R. White

THE ENGLISH BAPTISTS

OF THE

EIGHTEENTH CENTURY

Raymond Brown

The Baptist Historical Society

This is the second volume in a new series on the English Baptists originally planned under the editorship of the late Dr E. A. Payne and now edited by Dr B. R. White.

Already published

THE ENGLISH BAPTISTS OF THE SEVENTEENTH CENTURY

by B. R. White

In preparation

THE ENGLISH BAPTISTS OF THE NINETEENTH CENTURY

by J. H. Y. Briggs

Cover design by Jo Crabbe

© 1986   The Baptist Historical Society
                    4 Southampton Row, London, WC1B 4AB

ISBN 0 903166 10 0

THE ENGLISH BAPTISTS

OF THE

EIGHTEENTH CENTURY

(1689 - 1815)

CONTENTS

LIST OF ILLUSTRATIONS

The illustrations are taken from prints in Bristol Baptist College, unless otherwise stated.

Inside Cover: Eminent Baptists of the Eighteenth Century

Centre pages: Joseph Stennett
1663 – 1713

John Gill
1697 – 1771
From C. H. Spurgeon, *Autobiography I,*
1899

Robert Robinson
1735 – 1790
Print in possession of the Revd Roger
Hayden

Caleb Evans
1737 – 1791

Dan Taylor
1738 – 1816
Print in possession of Queensbury Baptist
Church, Bradford

Andrew Fuller
1754 – 1815

Robert Hall
1764 – 1831

William Steadman
1764 – 1837

Photography by Brian Bowers

AUTHOR'S NOTE

Readers of the first volume in this series[1] will be aware that during the first two centuries of their history, English Baptists consisted of two 'denominations'. Each with a distinctive ancestry, sharply divided by theology and, to a lesser degree, practice, General (Arminian) and Particular (Calvinistic) Baptist churches had very limited contact with each other before the early nineteenth century. In order to minimise the possibility of confusion I have, after an introductory chapter, related the story of General and Particular Baptist life in alternate chapters. My debt to scholars and historians of English dissent will be apparent throughout but, in addition, I wish to acknowledge with special gratitude the help I have received from Faith Bowers, Audrey Jones, Geoffrey Nuttall, Paul Richards, Barrie White, and my wife, Christine. I would like to dedicate the book to the members of Spurgeon's College Council as an expression of my warm thanks for so much kindness and support during my Principalship over the past thirteen years.

RAYMOND BROWN

September 1986

[1] B. R. White, *The English Baptists of the Seventeenth Century*, 1983.

THE ENGLISH BAPTISTS

OF THE

EIGHTEENTH CENTURY

1

'Expectation of Great Things'

Once it became known that James II had left their shores, English dissenters breathed a sigh of relief. For them, the accession of William and Mary initiated a new era, encouraging both the General and Calvinistic (Particular) Baptists gratefully to anticipate a brighter future. A number of issues continued to claim their attention as, with differing emphases but common concerns, the two distinct groups of Baptist people looked towards the new century.

First, they had clearly arrived at a time of dramatic *political* change. William of Orange had landed in England intent on using the new monarchy as a further check on French expansionism and both king and queen had come jointly to the throne as convinced Protestants. Deeply persuaded both of God's sovereignty and man's freedom, William III made no secret of his deep religious convictions. The contemporary historian, Gilbert Burnet, knew that William's Calvinism was no mere credal formality; the new king was 'much possessed with the belief of absolute decrees'.[1] William was also convinced that in order for his rule to be effective and his opposition to France strengthened, the grievances of the people must be minimised and the nation united. More than one English politician was of the firm view that toleration in Holland had been one of the reasons for that country's economic prosperity. Dissenters, therefore, must have liberty to worship as they wished and not as Parliamentary legislation demanded. Earlier restrictions on their freedom were speedily removed, though not without opposition. Many Anglican clergy were affronted that England's new king was not only 'zealous for toleration' but generously indifferent about matters like 'forms of church government'. Relieved of most of the penalties imposed by the Clarendon Code, Baptists shared in the general rejoicing. After almost thirty years of intermittent hardship and persecution, they were glad that they had lived to see such a dramatic transformation. The

1

Toleration Act meant that, once again, they could meet freely, no longer threatened by well-rewarded informers or irate magistrates. The new reign, with its revised legislation for dissent, 'put a new life in those who before were sunk in despair'.[2] It was a time for confident growth. In the twenty years which followed the accession of William and Mary, over 3,000 licences were issued to dissenters,[3] though it has to be remembered that a congregation might register several homes as places for occasional meetings. Expansion of this kind made many Anglicans distinctly uneasy.

Baptists knew only too well that their freshly-won privileges were precariously held. Toleration might easily be withdrawn. Burnet was aware that some of his fellow Anglicans showed 'an implacable hatred to the nonconformists' yet, despite some highly vocal clerical opposition, there were, all over the land, 'wise and good men who did very much applaud' freedom for dissenters. William himself believed that 'conscience was God's province and that it ought not to be imposed on'. His experience in Holland 'made him look on toleration as one of the wisest measures of government'.[4] Throughout the eighteenth century Baptists and their nonconformist colleagues kept an alert eye on matters affecting their religious freedom. What they had gained might quickly disappear. With a different king the scene could change dramatically. When William died, the General Baptist preacher, Joseph Jenkins, rejoiced that 'our liberties are not lost with our prince',[5] but during the reign of Anne there were constant attempts to inhibit the progress of dissent. Strenuous efforts were made, for example, to check the increasing nonconformist presence in the boroughs by attacking the practice of 'occasional conformity'. On two occasions in November 1697 one 'occasional conformer', London's Lord Mayor, Sir Humprey Edwin, attended Sunday afternoon Dissenters' services in full mayoral regalia after he had worshipped at a parish church in the morning.[6] Highly respected Tory politicians like William Bromley regarded such conduct as 'abominable hypocrisy' and 'inexcusable immorality'.[7]

Moreover, it was passionately maintained that everything possible must be done to curtail the considerable educational and, it was feared, political influence of the Dissenting Academies. John Wesley's father, Samuel, had studied at an Academy in Newington Green. Later, in making a bid for preferment, he complained in print not only about their 'mortal aversion to the Episcopal order', but also that some with their 'king-killing doctrines equally abhorred monarchy itself'. [8] Nonconformity was rarely without vociferous enemies at any time in the century. At the time of the Jacobite rebellion in 1745 the Independent minister, Philip Doddridge, acknowledged the highly tentative nature of their freedom. He knew how easily the Dissenters might lose the liberties they had enjoyed since the accession of William III: 'We have long enjoyed halcyon days', but 'how soon clouds may gather'. He feared that some of nonconformity's 'younger brethren may live to see ... our religious liberties trampled under foot, and with them undoubtedly our civil, for they are twins that will live and die together'. [9] Over thirty years later the Particular Baptist leader, Robert Robinson (1735-90), wrote his *Plan of Lectures* as a teaching-aid for those who wanted to instruct young people concerning 'the principles of nonconformity'. He was at pains to emphasise the importance of religious liberty. At the close of the century his successor at Cambridge, Robert Hall, Jnr (1764-1831), was concerned not simply to guard their privileged freedom, but also to remove such inequalities which stubbornly remained.

Secondly, Baptists soon realised that they had entered a period of *religious* ferment. Two issues were never removed from their agenda of doctrinal debate - an external threat, Roman Catholicism, and an internal pressure, Rationalism.

According to the Particular Baptist preacher, Benjamin Stinton (1677-1719), the 'unhappy King James II' had earnestly 'attempted the subversion of our laws' and 'the restoration of Popery' in order to 'enslave us to a foreign prince and an arbitrary power'. When Queen Anne died, Stinton regretfully acknowledged that there had been several occasions in her reign when a threatened change of policy might easily have led to the removal of 'civil and religious privileges'. The dissenters and their children might well have been 'left to inherit nothing but popery and slavery'. Stinton was relieved that, with the coronation of George I, such 'deep laid designs' were overthrown and the 'Protestant succession' firmly established by the House of Hanover. With the new king's reign, Stinton believed that the 'hopes of a Pretender are entirely cut off; no foreign power daring yet to give him any assistance'. [10]

Dissenting patriotism in the eighteenth century has this anti-Catholic polemic as one of its most prominent strands. Moreover, the fear of Rome was far from being a distinctively nonconformist neurosis. [11] Anglicans also shared the view that, if James II had been allowed to pursue his international policies without hindrance, it might well have led to the gradual demise of Protestantism. [12] Louis XIV's revocation (1685) of the Edict of Nantes had confirmed the average Englishman's worst suspicion that Catholicism and freedom were incompatible partners. The liberties earlier guaranteed to French Protestants had been cruelly withdrawn. Could any Catholic king keep his promises? William's military campaigns were a costly exercise and for a large part of his reign he was on the continent fighting alongside his troops. But in the popular mind, it was not simply a war for England; it was part of an essential struggle against Popery and oppression.

The 'loyal address', presented by nonconformist leaders on numerous occasions in the eighteenth century, was utterly genuine, but it must be remembered that the dissenters' submission to the monarchy was always conditional. Loyalty to God was paramount. John Piggott (died 1713) told his fellow Baptists that 'no pretence of allegiance or duty will justify our trust in a prince whose visible conduct declares his defiance to heaven, and whose arts of government are levelled against the laws of God'. Should a king 'once break his coronation oath and invade the liberties of his people, he is no longer a prince but a tyrant'. Piggott quoted William Wake, later Archbishop of Canterbury, that a king who governs 'only by the arbitrary motions of his own will' is 'no king of our acknowledging... nor did we ever oblige ourselves to obey such a one'. [13] If a king, like James II, appeared intent on thrusting Catholicism on the nation, then dissenters and Anglicans alike were determined to resist him.

At the beginning of our period the Dissenters' native fear of popery was kept alive by popular descriptive literature concerning the plight of the French Protestants. John Claude's *Account of the Persecutions and Oppressions of the Protestants in France* (1686) was extensively circulated during the reign of James. Substantial pamphlets of this kind served as vital propaganda within dissent, keeping their readers alert to the dangers of Catholicism. Preaching after the unsuccessful attempt on the life of William III, John Piggott says that if the king had been assassinated:

> how much worse had it been with us... who must have exchanged our liberties and laws for the usurping tyranny and slavery of France, and instead of singing this day, the tears of our widows and fatherless children might have been mixed with the ashes of our

city, and our streets floated with a stream of human blood.[14]

As the century moved on, warnings about 'Popery' continued to appear in Baptist preaching[15] but, serious as such polemical issues were, Baptists were to encounter a more sinister force within their own ranks. Eighteenth-century rationalism was more perilous than Roman Catholicism. The publication of books like John Toland's *Christianity not Mysterious* (1696) began to popularise the philosophy of John Locke and others who had insisted that the attention of Christian thinkers had been narrowly focused on 'revelation' to the comparative neglect of 'reason'. For some, convictions of this kind led steadily to deism and ultimately, in many cases, to the abandonment of revelation altogether. The supernatural dimension of the Christian faith gradually became an intellectual embarrassment. Increasingly there were those who considered good behaviour more important than orthodox belief and the universal plea for exemplary moral conduct began to displace the quest for personal salvation.

The preference for rationalistic proof had opposite effects within the life of the Baptists. In General Baptist churches it caused some to challenge conventional Christology and Trinitarian doctrine, whilst among the Particular Baptists it led to an intensification of their distinctive convictions so that they interpreted the doctrines of predestination and election with occasionally frightening logic. Much that they rightly maintained about the divine initiative in human redemption came to be presented within a rigid quasi-rationalistic framework, seriously distorting the doctrine of grace. A preoccupation with election caused some Particular Baptists in the eighteenth century to minimise the church's evangelistic imperative; it became theologically improper to invite unbelievers to respond to the claims of Christ. Only those predestined to salvation could believe, so an 'invitation' to personal faith appeared to deny the doctrine of election. Among some of the 'high Calvinists' who held such views, the 'rational' consequence of their teaching was that if the elect are eternally chosen and secure, moral conduct was of minimal consequence. These 'antinomians' maintained that just as good behaviour could not procure salvation, neither could bad conduct put it at risk. Dissenters who propagated ethically indifferent views of this kind were always in a minority, but their extreme teaching was a persistent worry to those genuine 'high Calvinists' who constantly asserted the importance of 'law' as well as of 'grace'.

Thirdly, like other Christians, Baptists became increasingly concerned in this century about the evident *moral* decline in English society. From the Restoration period onwards a serious deterioration was evident both in ethical ideals and everyday conduct. Many believers, not only Baptists, blamed the theatre; these 'academies of hell' and 'nurseries of all vice' were notoriously evil.[16] Whitelocke Bulstrode maintained that 'one playhouse ruins more souls than fifty churches are able to save'.[17] Gilbert Burnet grieved that many of the people who were 'deeply corrupted in principle' had boasted 'a disbelief of revealed religion and a profane mocking of the Christian faith and the mysteries of it'. He feared that 'the nation was falling under such a general corruption, both as to morals and to principles', that it gave 'great apprehensions of heavy judgments from heaven'.[18] Many Christians of orthodox belief regarded the devastating storm of 1703, in which many hundreds of Europeans lost their lives, as evidence of God's displeasure. The plague (1665), London's great fire (1666)[19] and subsequent earthquake (1691) were similarly thought to be signs of divine warning. For several decades 'storm' sermons were preached annually[20] in which congregations were urged to repent, avert the wrath of God, abandon their unworthy behaviour and turn dependently to Christ. Loose living would end in eternal judgement.

Moral indifference was evident throughout all classes of society. In the late seventeenth century the Particular Baptist minister, Benjamin Keach (1640-1704) complained that 'profane swearers and cursed blasphemers' were constantly heard in London's streets, people 'who daily belch out most abominable oaths, calling upon the holy and patient God to *Damn them* every day'. Drunkenness too was common at this time. Keach grieved that inebriated men and women were seen 'reeling along the streets' whilst 'a multitude of common harlots' were a further 'shame of this city and nation'.[21] Moral outrage of this kind was not limited to irate preachers, Baptist or otherwise. The royal proclamations of William III, Mary and Anne gave frequent expression to wide concern. Soon after his arrival in London, William wrote to his two archbishops and the bishop of London urging that the clergy 'preach frequently against those particular sins and vices which are most prevailing in this realm' and remind their congregations of 'such statute law or laws as are provided against blasphemy, swearing and cursing, perjury, drunkenness and profanation of the Lord's Day'.[22] Such royal proclamations were to be read in churches four times a year and displayed in conspicuous public places throughout the land. Archbishop Thomas Tenison gave voice to the concern of many Christians when he told his fellow bishops that 'the sensible growth of vice and profaneness' would surely 'bring down the heaviest judgments of God' upon the nation. [23]

Despite their evident alarm about declining moral standards, Baptists did not give significant support to the rapidly proliferating Societies for the Reformation of Manners. The General Baptist, Joseph Burroughs (1685-1765), and the Particular Baptist ministers, Samuel Wilson (1702-50) and Andrew Gifford, Jnr (1700-84), were unusual in this respect. Most General Baptists were rigidly insular, reluctant to identify with other denominations whatever the issue, whilst Particular Baptists, preoccupied with doctrinal controversy, were frequently neglectful of contemporary moral and social issues. At this time some Anglican ministers were urging their colleagues to 'let alone the mysterious points of religion' and to preach 'only good, plain, practical morality'. [24] Acceptable conduct became more important than doctrinal orthodoxy.

As the new century progressed, a number of leading General Baptists began to give increasing, and later almost exclusive, dominance to moral issues in their pulpit ministry. James Foster (1697-1753) became typical of a growing number of General Baptist preachers for whom insistence on theological freedom went hand in hand with moralistic preaching. Ministers of this kind identified warmly with sentiments like those popularly expressed by Alexander Pope:

> For modes of faith, let graceless zealots fight,
> His can't be wrong whose life is in the right. [25]

In a period of widespread moral decay, ethical preaching was certainly necessary, but the New Testament message offered a redemptive power which some of these preachers tended to ignore.

Fourthly, the eighteenth-century Baptist scene was characterised by *ecclesiastical* controversy. Seemingly irreconcilable theological positions separated friends and divided congregations. But it was hardly a distinctively Baptist peculiarity. Highly important doctrinal issues were constantly under discussion in *all* the main Christian

Communions. Without this perspective, eighteenth-century Baptists may appear unusually quarrelsome and divisive. In 1704 John Piggott preached to London Particular Baptists about Christian unity. He reminded them of the quarrels between Jansenists and Jesuits, between Franciscans and Dominicans, between the Gallican church 'and those that are more enslaved to the Bishop of Rome in Italy and Spain'. Fierce controversy was part of the general ecclesiastical scene. In surveying the highly contentious features of contemporary Catholicism, Piggott was in no sense complacent. 'It's lawful to learn from an enemy', he said, and went on to remind his hearers of the need for creative peace within the life of the Baptist people. He invited them realistically to acknowledge that, coming from a variety of different backgrounds, 'it is not probable we should concur exactly in all the same opinions'. Surely, 'for one Christian to censure and condemn another merely because he cannot agree with him in small or indifferent things, is as unreasonable as for one man to quarrel with the rest of the world, because they have not his features and complexion'. Piggott is no advocate of doctrinal indifference: 'Charity itself will not allow us to associate and unite with those whose doctrines sap the foundation of the Christian religion'. But the preacher knows that there are certainly a number of matters 'that are less clearly revealed' or are 'indifferent in their own nature' and in these cases there is no reason why 'our different apprehensions in lesser matters' should 'abate our mutual respects'.

The context and occasion of Piggott's sermon is important; it was preached in the presence of 'several congregations assembled together'[26] at a crucial time in the history of the Particular Baptists. After a decade of quarrelsome relationships, mainly over hymn-singing, serious attempts were now in hand to revive the 'London Association', an assembly of church representatives from many parts of south-eastern England, the home counties, some northern counties and London itself. Piggott and others had experienced the pain and witnessed the cost of factious controversy. The divisive arguments of an unharmonious decade had robbed the Particular Baptists of any meaningful national identity.

It is essential, however, to look beyond denominational boundaries, for among dissenters at large relationships were often difficult. The bright promise of 1691, the 'Happy Union' of Presbyterians and Independents, came to an abrupt end within eight years. The two denominations encountered serious disagreements about doctrine and practice. The Independents were exposed to criticism about itinerant lay preaching. [27] Presbyterians became more seriously divided over Trinitarian doctrine, and Quakers over the subtle infiltration of deism.

Quarrelsome tendencies were not confined to dissent. Priests were divided over their attitude to those parishioners who preferred the meeting-house to the parish church. Some Anglicans were not in the least resentful that the nonconformists had their freedom, but there were others, like the Tory pamphleteer, Sir Roger L'Estrange, who regarded all dissenters as potential revolutionaries: 'toleration of religion is cousin germane to a licence for rebellion'. [28] Churchmen also argued among themselves over loyalty to the Stuarts. In 1688 some High Church bishops including Sancroft of Canterbury, and over 400 clergy, refused to take the oath of allegiance to the new king, but before long these 'non-jurors' were themselves fragmented by internal controversy. The episcopate was divided between Whigs and Tories. In these circumstances there was always the danger that political allegiance could drive yet another wedge between churchmen of varying shades and opinions.

Piggott's sermon emphasised that serious divisions were hardly a Protestant monopoly. Fenelon's quietism was strenuously opposed by Bossuet, and Burnet may have been right in suggesting that their quarrels were not solely theological: 'A rivalry for favour and preferment had as great a share in it, as zeal for the truth'. [29]

Baptists of this period forcefully debated such diverse topics as hymn-singing, marriage outside the congregation, Christology, election, evangelism, antinomianism, Socinianism, open and closed communion. Such issues were not in fact peripheral to the life of eighteenth-century people whatever their denominational allegiance. For many of them Christian faith was inseparably woven into the fabric of everyday life. It was not an easily disposable commodity of marginal significance. When contrary views were expressed, some aspect of the believer's obedience to God may well have been challenged or, more seriously, even his eternal security. It is hardly surprising that feelings ran high.

Finally, Baptists throughout our period were naturally influenced by their *social* environment. During most of the eighteenth century nearly 80% of England's population lived in rural areas and the majority owed their livelihood to agriculture or were employed in the production of the countryside's raw materials. At the beginning of the century, one in eight Englishmen lived in London. Norwich was the next largest city, followed by Bristol, then Exeter, York, Newcastle, Colchester and Yarmouth, each of which boasted a population of about 10,000. In 1700 the national population numbered about five million, most of whom saw nothing of the country's gradually expanding cities.

Sociological factors are of immense importance in tracing the story of the eighteenth-century Baptists. Most churches were in rural areas; insularity was inevitable. In many parts of the country travel was exceptionally difficult. Poorly maintained highways, virtually impassable in bad weather, hindered communication, whilst such roads as were kept in reasonable condition were constantly frequented by highwaymen.[30] People with business or professional interests naturally made long journeys, increasingly so as the century progressed, but travel was never an enviable experience. In London's Hyde Park a gunman shot at Horace Walpole, who later maintained that 'one is forced to travel, even at noon, as if one was going to battle'.[31]

Wealthy people were scarce among the Baptists so most members of these congregations saw little of England beyond their neighbouring villages and the local market town. For this reason alone, the gradual development and increasing vigour of association life throughout the eighteenth century was a remarkable achievement. It helped to break down the inevitable isolation and served to minimise the inter-congregational pettiness which sometimes characterised the life of people whose horizons rarely extended beyond their local boundaries.

The average normal size of Baptist congregations may not have exceeded fifty, though there were impressive exceptions. The information collected for the Compton Census (1676) indicates that some towns had dissenting congregations of several hundreds. In the records of early eighteenth-century journeys made by Celia Fiennes and Daniel Defoe, the reader frequently stumbles across details of well-packed meeting-houses, but both those travellers were predisposed to nonconformity and their impressions may not be entirely objective. Dissent was numerically strong in London, and a number of towns had well-supported congregations, but its main adherents were scattered throughout the hamlets, villages and small market-towns of the English countryside. Alan Everitt has illustrated the point from the sales of Philip Doddridge's popular *Family Expositor*, widely used for devotional reading throughout eighteenth-century Dissent; at least two-thirds of the subscribers to the first volume were from a rural or semi-rural environment. He has also shown that 'outside London at least one half and probably two-thirds of all English dissenters before 1740 were countrymen and not townsmen'.[32] It must also be remembered that in any locality the inner core of committed members was always surrounded by a far larger number of regular adherents who, for a variety of reasons, baulked at the responsibilities of church membership.

In the closing decades of the eighteenth century, the Particular Baptist minister, Benjamin Francis (1734-99) says that his congregation in the Gloucestershire parish of Horsley 'in general are poor, plain' people who 'have not had the advantage of literature' and have never been part of a 'genteel congregation'. He contrasts them sharply with 'an intelligent and polite congregation in a city',[33] but was content to stay with them, even through periods of financial hardship, because of his genuine pastoral concern and their mutual affection. At a time when he was confronted with the possibility of moving to Carter Lane, Southwark, as successor to the high Calvinist, John Gill, he told his friend Caleb Evans (1737-91): 'The thought of parting with my dear people, and of the unhappy consequences that may follow, dissolves my heart, and almost overpowers my spirits... I do not expect to be more happy... than I am at present: they love me exceedingly, as I also do them'.[34]

The church Francis served in rural Gloucestershire was typical of Baptist life throughout most of this century. It had its roots in an agrarian society with stability, dependability, integration, continuity and insularity as part of its mingled strength and weakness. Generations of inter-marrying meant that members of such churches were closely related. Lay leadership was often confined to privileged families who had served for many generations. The closeness provided strength, but under the care of ministers less gifted than Benjamin Francis, the church's horizons could become limited. Corporate life might degenerate into self-regarding independence, even doctrinaire superiority.

In his *History of my own Times* Burnet says that the accession of William III 'drew upon it an universal expectation of great things to follow, from such auspicious beginnings'. The bishop shared the delight of thousands that 'so general a joy'[35] was so widely spread throughout the country. Baptists were relieved and grateful but not, as might have been expected, correspondingly zealous in evangelism. Almost three decades of intermittent persecution had exhausted their strength. Physically tired and emotionally drained, they were only too glad to be left in peace. In the first half of the new century, with rare exceptions, congregations strengthened the walls of defensive isolation. Their confessional ecclesiology frequently allegorised Old Testament imagery, portraying the local church as a 'garden enclosed'.[36] They rarely remembered that in the Canticles the invigorating wind would blow upon the garden so that fragrant spices could 'flow out'. Most General Baptists became preoccupied with introspective archaisms, whilst many of their Particular Baptist contemporaries were to argue with tiresome monotony whether it was ever fitting to offer an invitation to saving faith. The late seventeenth-century 'expectation of great things' did not immediately issue in effective mission on any meaningful scale and it was not until the closing decades of the new century that churches of both groups were diverted from arid controversy to fruitful expansion.

* * * * * * * *

FREEDOM   1689 – 1730

'Against clear light'

In the early summer of 1689, General Baptists greeted the new era by meeting in London for a deliberative assembly. Appointed delegates from 'many parts' of the nation came to discuss the life and work of their scattered congregations. With new, if limited, freedom secured, at least temporarily, by the Toleration Act, they were presented with a unique opportunity not only for consolidation but vigorous expansion. Harsh restrictions imposed by the Clarendon Code were now a thing of the past, only occasionally recalled in funeral sermons with their recollection of courageous leadership in dark times. No longer inhibited by oppressive legislation, the General Baptists of 1689 now had the chance not only to defend their doctrine of universal redemption but to apply it practically to contemporary spiritual and moral needs. Thomas Grantham (1634-93), the Lincolnshire Messenger, was their most gifted leader. His extensive writings had been widely circulated among the churches during the Restoration period, but his evangelistic plea seems to have fallen on deaf ears. In his view

> the most glorious and worthy work to be done by God's people, is to advance his truth, and to seek the salvation of the world, by all possible means... all is but trifles in comparison... A necessity was laid upon Paul to preach the gospel; it's strange no man should be under a necessity now!... Men are in as great danger to be lost to eternity as then; there is therefore a necessity that the gospel be faithfully preached now as well as then. [1]

By the beginning of the new reign, Grantham was in his mid-fifties. Earlier imprisonment, tiring journeys and exacting ministry within introspective communities may well have proved disheartening, even for a robust leader like him. The 1689 Assembly made him responsible for summarizing its findings, but his record provides little evidence of spiritual vigour within the congregations. The topics under discussion betray introverted preoccupation. 'Diverse letters' from their churches in several counties shared as their main concern 'how they should demean themselves towards those who have married or shall marry out of the bounds' of General Baptist churches. Although the issue was 'largely debated' throughout the second day of the Assembly and 'all endeavours used to find out some larger bounds than the said community', the representatives came firmly to the conclusion that it was perilous to 'exceed those bounds'. The narrow denominationalism of the General Baptists in this period is reflected in their decision that prospective matrimony is denied not only to 'Turks, Jews [and] Infidels' but also to 'all sorts of pretended Christians'. The Assembly insisted that the Pauline marriage restriction (II Corinthians 6.14-18) is meant to define an unbeliever as anyone who 'is not a member of the visible Church of Christ'. Offenders who had married outside 'the baptised churches' were to be treated with some leniency 'that justice and mercy may meet together', but prohibitions of this kind, which accused all other denominations of pretence, can hardly have improved their already tenuous relationships with other Christians.

The discussion of the Assembly representatives moved from marriage to music. The singing of metrical psalms was the next item on their agenda, the main problem being whether it was fitting for Christians to mingle their voices with those of unbelievers. Such novel practices as congregational singing were dismissed as 'carnal formalities'. An appointed soloist might be encouraged to sing some verses representatively just as one member might lead a congregation in prayer. Singers were reminded that just 'as a mournful voice becomes the duty of prayer so a joyful voice with gravity becomes the duty of praising God with a song in the Church of God'. As he closed his account of the 1689 proceedings Grantham wrote that the 'Assembly concluded in peace'. In that respect it was to become almost unique. Its delegates had seriously debated the topic of singing but, as they left for home, there was little for them to sing about, either individually or collectively. This first occasion for a national Assembly for over twenty years hardly encouraged optimism and became a sad prototype of General Baptist life in the early eighteenth century.[2]

In examining the continuing work of these churches in this period it is important to discern why, over several decades, they suffered such evident deterioration. From the Restoration onwards, several factors combined to inhibit the healthy development of their congregational life. Why were they unable to respond adventurously to the challenge of a new opportunity?

First of all, contemporary statistics indicate that, from a numerical point of view alone, General Baptists were seriously disadvantaged. In the early eighteenth century their attendance figures were less than half of their Particular Baptist contemporaries. From the information gathered in 1715-18 by the London Presbyterian minister John Evans, it is estimated that a total of almost 19,000 'hearers' were found in about 120 General Baptist congregations, whereas 206 Particular Baptist churches had over 40,000.

Furthermore, their geographical distribution was severely limited. In many respects, General Baptists at the beginning of this period were little more than a 'Home Counties' movement with limited additional support from a few more distant counties. Relatively strong in Kent, Sussex, Buckinghamshire and Cambridgeshire, their most distant outposts were Lincolnshire in the East, Wiltshire and Somerset in the West. Geographical locations may owe something to their ancestry, the Lincolnshire strength to John Smyth's Gainsborough connections in the early seventeenth century, the Home Counties, especially Buckinghamshire, to a line that can be traced through recurrent family names to pre-Reformation Lollardy.[3] Particular Baptists, on the other hand, were more widely distributed, covering most of the English counties south of the Midlands and reaching into the southern half of Wales. The restricted geographical distribution of the General Baptists naturally precluded a more vigorous and creative exchange of ideas with people exposed to different influences.

It is possible that General Baptists may also have been hindered in their development in this period because of their reluctance or inability to build a meeting-house. Once a small church was established it may have seemed pointless to pour their limited resources into a costly building programme. Rural communities already provided adequate meeting places for their seventeenth-century congregations. Farmers were among the earliest leaders and a large farmhouse or suitably equipped barn was easily placed at the disposal of members. During the years of persecution such meeting places were safely off the beaten track, left unharassed by avaricious or vindictive informers, and a sympathetic local magistrate might readily turn a blind eye to the fact that relatively small numbers met regularly for worship on farm premises. The church where Matthew Caffyn (1628-1715) was minister had a number of meeting places 'in and about Horsham' and two farms which he rented at Southwater and Broadbridge Heath were regularly used for meetings. This Sussex church was established before the Restoration and, although land was purchased for a meeting-house, none was built until the early 1720s. By that time the Horsham General Baptists had been meeting in farms for 65 years. The church at Horley in Surrey met in members' homes for a century.[4] Likewise the church in the Kent hamlet of Bessels Green had no meeting-house until 1716; before the time of the Civil War its members were drawn from surrounding villages in the Weald and private houses used for their meetings. Here again, an important church was without a meeting-house for about 75 years.[5]

A similar story can be told of the General Baptists in Cambridgeshire who were glad to use the farm at Caxton Pastures for their worship.[6] It was some time before separate meeting places were erected for the use of members who lived in various parts of the county. Naturally, the persecution period put a stop to any building plans which may have been in mind prior to the restrictive legislation of the Clarendon Code, but even when some measure of toleration came, and General Baptist congregations had an opportunity to build, it was sometimes a quarter of a century before they did so. London churches might well be able to purchase vacant premises and do what the High Hall church did in 1699 and take over a building formerly used by the Independents.[7] But it was not so easy in the provinces. In 1698 the Norwich members, financially embarrassed and 'indebted about forty pounds for the building of their meeting place which they are not able to pay', sought the help of other General Baptists. These believers were anxious that their debt was 'likely to be very prejudicial to the interest of Christ' in the city and other General Baptist churches were asked to help 'very speedily'.[8]

Urgent pleas of this kind discouraged churches from embarking on projects beyond their means. Although the practice of using farms, barns and houses for their meetings may have been an economic necessity, in other respects it may have hindered their development. The provision of a meeting-house encouraged congregational stability, fostered a sense of continuity and helped to ensure that the church had a secure base for its future witness. Dependence on prosperous farmers like Caffyn, or other leaders with spacious homes, might not always work in the church's favour. The family which generously provided the meeting place might too rigidly determine its policy, and the members could be robbed of healthy independence. When divisive issues were tabled for debate, impartial and unfettered judgment could be difficult. It was important for members to meet on neutral ground, their gatherings dignified by a bond of equal privilege as well as shared responsibility. In such circumstances small numbers, insular attitudes and inhibited members all combined to stifle if not silence creative discussion.

In this enclosed type of community, old assumptions and unexamined traditions were rarely questioned. Antique patterns of life and work were continued without significant challenge. These traditional General Baptist practices need to be examined carefully. Each claimed biblical precedent, but several were lifted from the pages of scripture without much regard to either their contextual setting or contemporary relevance. In several places the dietary laws adopted by the Council of Jerusalem (Acts 15) became a traditional aspect of General Baptist prohibition; several congregations discouraged eating 'blood' with little appreciation of its first century context. We have referred already to their disapproval of psalm-singing by a congregation of worshippers. A literal interpretation of biblical passages often forced them into controversy and division on what appear to us to be marginal issues.

General Baptists of an earlier generation defended the necessity of evening communion services simply because it is the Lord's *Supper*.[9] Their successors later discussed whether, because certain New Testament passages referred to elders in the plural, particular ordinances demanded more than one elder.[10] Foot washing continued to be practised in some congregations, even with divisive effects, and the anointing of the sick in accordance with James 5, however appropriate, gave rise to further contention. When in 1724 the congregation at Sevenoaks enquired whether it was 'lawful and expedient' to repeat the Lord's Prayer in corporate worship, the assembly firmly discouraged its use 'since it is not the practice of the baptised churches' and its introduction might well become 'a burden or great scruple in the conscience of many of the members'.[11] It would be a mistake to assume that conservatism of this kind was confined to the General Baptists. In the same period Philip Doddridge was regarded as 'a legal preacher' because at Kibworth he had used 'such a rag of popery' as 'a form called the Lord's Prayer'.[12]

The General Baptist practice of the imposition of hands at baptism, 'for the gift of the promised Spirit', became a further controversial issue. The early eighteenth-century Messenger, Thomas Dean, asserted the necessity of 'two lawful administrators' at baptism so that the laying on of hands is 'administered jointly', while other congregations insisted that 'though but one of them lay hands upon a baptised believer it is sufficient'.[13] Pedantry and scrupulosity not only prevented the infiltration of new ideas; it isolated the General Baptists from many of their fellow dissenters as well as from churchmen.

Endogamy was a firmly rooted tradition which more seriously inhibited the gradual and natural introduction of fresh insights. The fact that the subject continued to be debated at most of their national assemblies suggests that at least some of their members rebelled against an entrenched policy. The highly controversial topic of marriage to a partner outside the insular fellowship of the General Baptist churches was constantly under review. Slightly over half the country's population was female in the eighteenth century and for decades frustrated sisters within these churches probably kept the topic alive and urgent. Prior to the 'glorious revolution' two London General Baptists entered into a pamphlet controversy on the subject. In 1681 Stephen Torey, the Stepney minister, published his *Mixed Marriages Vindicated* only to be criticized the following year by the Dunning's Alley minister, John Griffith (1622-1700), who vigorously supported the conventional view in *The Unlawfulness of Mixed Marriages*. Intermittent enquiries were tentatively, hopefully and frequently made by the representatives of the churches when they met in association or assembly, but the response was invariably the same. In 1702 the negative decision of the 1668 Assembly was explicitly repeated and upheld. To marry outside the fellowship is a 'sin' and, in the absence of 'unfeigned repentance', the offender 'ought to be withdrawn from'.[14]

Before hastily condemning this apparently harsh pattern of discipline, it is important to recognise that baptism and admission to membership of these churches included subscription to the local congregation's Covenant, which invariably contained a prohibition against 'marrying out'. A Chesham member, for example, was 'withdrawn from' in 1715 'for marrying contrary to the law of God and her Covenant in baptism'.[15]

In 1704 the Burnham-on-Crouch church raised this matter again in the assembly and, after 'considerable debate', it was agreed to stand by the decision made thirty-six years

19

earlier that, for a member to marry a partner other than a General Baptist was not only, initially, an offence 'against the law of God', but continues to be a 'sin' even after repentance if the couple insist on living together 'as a man and wife'. Even the terminology used in these discussions heightened the emotional stress. The 1668 assembly had agreed that to describe mixed marriages as 'fornication' might be considered extravagant but, in order to heal the division between those who objected to its use and those who believed it appropriate, it was concluded that individual members should affirm: 'Agreed that I shall not call it fornication to the trouble of my brother nor he say it is not fornication to trouble me'. Definitions were important in this area. The representatives were in no doubt that the offence is properly described as 'marrying out of the Lord or out of the Church'.[16]

In an attempt to answer a further enquiry from the Norwich church the assembly returned to the question fifteen years later. It re-stated the conviction that there is no biblical warrant for 'persons baptised to marry with those unbaptised'. The representatives agreed to urge 'ministers and others' to 'use their utmost endeavours to prevent such marriages' and so preserve 'the peace and unity of the churches'.[17]

At this stage there was little flexibility and the women suffered most. During the next twenty-five years the scene gradually changed but not without considerable personal distress and an unnecessary depletion of their membership. In 1744 one of their respected leaders asked whether a sister in one of their churches must refuse a proposal of marriage from a genuine Christian 'merely because he has not happened to be baptised by immersion or profession of faith'.[18] In the earlier years of the century, the use in this context of the word 'merely', and by a General Baptist Messenger, would have been unthinkable.

But even more seriously divisive issues than marriage were to mar 'the peace and unity of the churches'. The most contentious topic to be discussed in their assemblies was not domestic but doctrinal. The same passion for precise scriptural warrants was applied to theological ideas as well as distinctive practices. Some began to ask whether traditional beliefs about the person of Christ and the Trinity owed more to credal definitions than to the Bible. Radical questioning of this kind was certainly not peculiar to the General Baptists at this time.[19] In his influential and highly controversial book, *Scripture-doctrine of the Trinity* (1712), the rector of St James's, Piccadilly, Samuel Clarke, claimed to have examined all the relevant texts and emerged unconvinced about biblical authority for conventional Trinitarian doctrine. Among the General Baptists fierce controversy continued to centre upon the unorthodox Christology of the Sussex Messenger, Matthew Caffyn. Inability to reconcile divergent convictions concerning the person of Christ led to fatal divisions within the General Baptist churches. Although the denomination enjoyed some phases of temporary healing, the recurrent disruption weakened a community already far from robust. Serious theological differences aggravated a tension already present between, on the one hand, the Buckinghamshire and Hertfordshire churches, whose ancestry went back to Lollardy, and the Kent and Sussex churches who appear to have been influenced by unorthodox Christology such as that taught by the sixteenth-century Anabaptist leader, Melchior Hoffmann. Their identical baptismal convictions were of limited cohesive value if they could not agree on an issue as central as the person of Christ.

The Orthodox Creed of 1679, published on the initiative of the Buckinghamshire Messenger, Thomas Monk (1656-99), clearly opposed deviant Christology. Its preface affirmed that the denial of baptism 'is a less evil than to deny the divinity or humanity of Christ'.[20] But this credal affirmation was a local document adopted neither officially nor widely within the General Baptist churches. By 1693 congregations in Buckinghamshire, Essex and London expressed increasing concern about the spread of Christologies which appeared to undermine both Christ's essential deity (that 'He is not of the uncreated substance of the Father but God made Him a creature only') and His true humanity by suggesting that He did not take the 'flesh of the virgin Mary'. The assembly agreed that such views were 'universally owned to be an error' but, by a majority vote, Caffyn was acquitted of the charge of holding them.[21]

From this point on the ranks of the English General Baptists were constantly subjected to theological controversy and inevitable fragmentation. Caffyn maintained his unconventional ideas with inflexible tenacity for several decades and at the price of denominational unity. Tiny communities of this kind needed a strong interdependent identity but Caffyn's Christology, which was strongly maintained by the Sussex churches, introduced a serious division.

Faced with two major parties in direct conflict, the 1693 Assembly attempted a compromise: it condemned the heresy and protected the accused. The assembly did not meet for three years in the hope that the trouble might settle down. It was an empty dream. When the representative Messengers and leaders came to London for their 1696 meeting the divisive topic was placed on the agenda by the churches of the Western Association. They believed it essential to have a common mind concerning Christ's deity, but discussion was stifled.[22] Grieved that they had been silenced, a number of churches broke away from the assembly and from that year the disrupted life of the General Baptists became focused on two rival gatherings of church representatives, both holding their meetings in London, usually at precisely the same time of the year. Those who stood by Caffyn (mainly churches in Kent and Sussex) continued to be known as the General Assembly, while the new body, formed mostly from the churches of London, Buckinghamshire, Cambridgeshire and Essex, described themselves as the General Association. In an attempt to avoid further division the Assembly decided that, if the members insisted on debating such matters, they must be asked to frame their convictions in biblical language: in 'the controversy respecting the Trinity and the Christ of God' future discussions, 'whether publicly or privately' voiced, should be 'in Scripture words and terms and in no other terms'.[23]

Strenuous efforts were made to effect a reconciliation between the two parties. Representative committees from both bodies gave detailed thought to the problem but entirely without success. Attempts to formulate an agreed written statement expressing a united theological conviction proved equally fruitless. Disturbed by Caffyn's views, the General Assembly's member churches in Northamptonshire and Lincolnshire transferred their allegiance to the General Association.

In time, the two rival groups came together and for a five year period were again united as one body. But, later, the trouble returned and those churches which stood for a theologically orthodox Christology became a gradually shrinking minority. Even those whose teaching appeared to be beyond suspicion were affronted by any suggestion of subscribing to credal definitions or doctrinal articles. It is significant that at the Salters' Hall controversy[24] in 1719, all but two of the Particular Baptists present were happy to subscribe to a Trinitarian affirmation whilst only one of the General Baptists was prepared to do so. In several instances, resistance to subscription became the prelude to heterodoxy. People who refused to sign the articles came eventually to deny them and those General Baptists who were theologically uncertain ultimately became committed Unitarians. Several of their orthodox leaders realised that hesitant Christology or optional Trinitarianism did not simply endanger their unity: it undermined their message.

Theological disharmony was undoubtedly painful but in defining biblical doctrine they were at least recalling centralities. A far more exasperating feature of General Baptist life in this period is that some of the issues which dominated their thinking appear trivial. Several of the debates which took place in national assemblies reflect petty squabbles in local churches. When they came together much time was spent in verbal wrangles unworthy of responsible church leaders. Personality clashes in local congregations were given national prominence. Quarrels which ought to have been settled amicably either within churches or between local congregations were made issues of wider concern. Two neighbouring churches in London suffered from broken relationships because of an inadequate apology. The matter had already been discussed ineffectively at association level which, in itself, was an indication of local mistrust. It appears that a disciplined member from Goodman's Fields had rather vaguely expressed his regret in Church Meeting that he had 'offended the brethren', but his fellow-members were not satisfied. They wanted him to be much more specific about his sins. The delegates at the 1696 Assembly were treated to the story in tiresome detail. It seems that one of the offender's friends privately asked him about his regrets only to be told that he knew of 'no cause to be sorry'. Ignorant of this personal comment and only aware of the public apology, the nearby White's Alley church received him into their fellowship. After considering the problem the two congregations were urged by the assembly to settle their differences, the White's Alley people told to acknowledge their mistake and the offender ordered to make a wholehearted apology such as that originally 'enjoined him by [the] Aylesbury Association'. It is sad that representatives from several counties had to listen to the wearisome details of a pastoral problem which had divided two congregations only a mile or two apart. At the same Assembly the Goodman's Fields members went on to relate a further disagreement, this time with the members of the Park church in Southwark. [25]

As the years went by, the Assembly was frequently asked to arbitrate in other aspects of congregational and inter-church controversy. It is a painful story of bewildering estrangement and continuing distrust. Problems of this kind were not confined to the theologically indefinite Assembly; the rival and doctrinally convinced General Association became similarly preoccupied with peripheral domestic concerns. At their 1704 London meeting two metropolitan churches were accused of slighting one of the denomination's Messengers. Thomas Dean was offended because 'he thought himself not to be treated as he ought to have been'; he had clearly taken far too much notice of 'the speeches of particular persons'.[26] The fact that a difference of opinion of that nature had to be settled by representatives from different parts of the country reflects badly on the life of the churches and indicates how fragile their local relationships were.

Pettiness of this order, as well as more serious doctrinal division, inevitably issued in a fragmented denominational organisation. Such troubles would have been serious enough in any community, but divided loyalties were particularly disastrous among churches which were proud of their corporate identity and stressed the importance of unified action. The General Baptists regarded congregational independence as 'very dangerous and detrimental to the Churches'.[27] Their ecclesiology was primarily connexional. Without sacrificing the privileged responsibilities of the local church, they were historically committed to the concept of a mutually dependent fellowship of united congregations.

The troubles went on. In the summer of 1709 the Assembly met initially in the White's Alley church but its representatives quarrelled so fiercely that one section moved off *en bloc* and established an alternative assembly at the Dunning's Alley meeting.[28] The departed group claimed to be the authentic Assembly and subsequently wrote letters to the churches inviting their affiliation.

Occasional references to procedural matters in the denomination's records suggest that, with such a wide range of topics, doctrinal, domestic and personal, their debates were often heated. The 1710 Assembly rightly laid it down that anyone speaking in their gatherings must 'direct his discourse to the Chairman or, by leave, to him whose cause is in debate and that all breaking in and interruptions shall be rebuked by Moderators';[29] those who were required to preside at such meetings had been entrusted with a thankless task.

With theological controversies, pastoral tensions, and organisational problems, the General Baptists were clearly in need of wise leadership, but at the turn of the century they lost a number of elderly men whose long ministry had been an inspiration for decades. Gifted and courageous leaders were hard to replace. The Messenger Thomas Grantham, their most popular writer and apologist, died in 1691 after a lifetime of service in Lincolnshire and its neighbouring counties. Also in 1691 they were deprived of Thomas Monk, the Buckinghamshire Messenger, a leader who had applied his alert mind, writing gifts and pastoral zeal to the preservation of sound doctrine. John Griffith died in 1700. He was greatly respected, having spent fourteen years in prison during the great persecution. With his passing the General Baptists lost an able and greatly admired writer. The Kent Messenger, Joseph Wright (born 1623) died in 1703. Initially a close friend of Matthew Caffyn, Wright had come to see the danger of the new teaching and gave his later years to the defence of traditional Christology. These four ministers had been eager to keep the General Baptist people true to orthodox Christian doctrine. It was not easy to find men who would gain equal respect within denominational life.

The passing of elderly leaders was predictable. What nobody could possibly have foreseen was the departure from the General Baptist ranks of some able men who might have been their natural successors. At almost the same time as the passing of these earlier leaders, some younger ministers left the service of General Baptist churches and gave their allegiance to the Particular Baptists. In the late 1680s both Richard Adams and Richard Allen (died 1717) transferred their ministry from different General Baptist churches to the Particulars. In 1699 John Piggott, minister of the Bow Street General Baptist church in London, left them to join the Little Wild Street church, and was later to become one of the most well-read preachers among the Particular Baptists. Mark Key[30] left the General Baptists in 1702 and, after a period of service in Reading, returned to London as senior minister at the Devonshire Square church, actively encouraging General Baptist churches to adopt a Calvinistic theology. These were ministerial losses the General Baptists could ill afford.

Denominational isolation was a further weakness in this period. During these difficult years some of their leaders would have been helped by meaningful contacts with evangelical Christians of other traditions, especially within Dissent, but fraternization was firmly discouraged. Their declared Arminianism heightened the problem. Among dissenters the Quakers were Arminians, and partly because of this Friends had in many places drawn members away from the General Baptist churches. Their doctrinal convictions concerning universal redemption cut them off from most of their other nonconformist contemporaries for, whatever their other differences, large numbers of Presbyterians, Independents and Particular Baptists at least had their firm Calvinism in common. The isolation was felt most acutely by General Baptist ministers in London. Sheer proximity to other dissenters in nearby meeting-houses helped to encourage some links but they were rarely allowed to develop.

Benjamin Keach had left the General Baptists when he was in his early thirties and had become one of the most dynamic and colourful ministers among the London Particular Baptists with a national reputation as preacher, author and hymn-writer. Whenever Keach discussed Arminianism, or even the 'middle way' teaching of Richard Baxter, he did so with uncomprising ferocity. By contrast, his sons-in-law, the minister Benjamin Stinton and his deacon Thomas Crosby, convinced Calvinists as they were, maintained openly conciliatory relationships with the General Baptists of London. Crosby's *History of the English Baptists* was heavily dependent on material collected by his brother-in-law and minister, Stinton. Benjamin Stinton's manuscripts, written in this period, do everything possible to minimize the differences between the General and Particular Baptists and this characteristic is evident in Crosby's published history.[31] But men like Stinton and Crosby were few and far between. General Baptists were made to feel 'poor neighbours' among dissenters and frequently disregarded when a Baptist voice was needed in united ventures. Understandably, they expressed their disappointment that the Baptist representatives on the Committee for the Three Denominations, formed in 1702, were both Calvinists. When these two ministers, Joseph Stennett (1663-1713) and John Piggott, died they were replaced by another two Particular Baptists, Benjamin Stinton and Richard Allen. The avoidance of General Baptist nominees occasioned 'unpleasant feelings' and the incident gave rise to the suggestion that both General and Particular Baptist ministers in London might come together for a monthly fraternal in the Hanover Coffee House in order to encourage 'a better union and correspondence between themselves'.[32] The well-respected General Baptist minister Joseph Jenkins was appointed Secretary but the venture was short-lived. Crosby was persuaded that if lay leaders had also been invited it might well have survived to encourage better relationships between the two groups.[33]

In 1717 another series of events took place in London which caused the General Baptist ministers in the city to feel even more isolated. Despite strenuous efforts by influential leaders like Stinton and the generous layman, Thomas Hollis (1659-1731), General Baptists were firmly excluded from the management and benefits of what came to be known as the Particular Baptist Fund. Its purpose was to provide young prospective ministers with a theological education by meeting the cost of essential books, and also give financial support to the many poor ministers in the Particular Baptist churches. Stinton pointed out that to refuse either financial help for or practical assistance from General Baptists would create an unfortunate impression within Dissent. After all, the Presbyterians also had a similar fund for helping ministers and, refusing to be narrowly partisan, had gladly helped both Independents and Baptists. Did the Particular Baptists wish to appear less tolerant and generous than their Calvinistic friends in the other denominations? But Stinton's well-argued plea for General Baptist participation in the fund came to nothing.[34] The later Salters' Hall debate (1719) and the submerged division within Dissent which it publicly exposed explains in part why the fund's managers were so resistant to the admission of General Baptists. They were more afraid of Arianism than Arminianism. After all, however orthodox some of their London ministers might be, some General Baptists made no secret of their doubts concerning the deity and humanity of Christ as well as the doctrine of the Trinity. Just as Stinton had used persuasive arguments in an attempt to include the General Baptists, so Thomas Hollis used his money. He offered further financial help if the Barbican church, of which he was a member, could be allowed to support the enterprise. This church in Paul's Alley had long been suspect because of its policy in accommodating members with both General and Particular Baptist sympathies. Hollis's offer was firmly rejected. Subsequent ministries at the Barbican church were to lend support to the managers' decision not to include the General Baptists for the church gradually moved from a conventional theology to a pattern of heterodox teaching which would have horrified its early ministers.

The alienation experienced even by doctrinally orthodox General Baptists at the beginning of the century was in part a self-inflicted wound. For many years they had openly discouraged friendly contact with other Christians. It ought not to have surprised them when fellow-Dissenters left them severely alone. At least two factors contributed to the isolation, their adversarial literature and their disciplinary legislation.

Gifted writers within the life of the General Baptist churches sometimes chose to devote their literary talents to denominational polemics. Only a few months before his death, Thomas Grantham published his *Dialogue between the Baptist and the Presbyterian* (1691). It was a fierce attack, not on Presbyterian churchmanship but on the 'cruel and soul-devouring doctrines' of Calvinism. With uncompromising language he decried the Presbyterians' teaching about predestination and election, with occasional caricatures of their treasured ideas. He did not live to see how it would be received by other denominations but it can have done little to endear the General Baptists to their Calvinistic contemporaries.

Far more serious were the restrictive resolutions passed by both the General Assembly and General Association concerning the relationship of their people with other Christians. We have already seen that marriage to a believer from another tradition was prohibited. The leaders also frowned on any form of contact with Christians outside their own ranks. They were certainly not free to attend other churches. A Chesham member was disciplined for passing 'by the place of his own meeting to go to hear the organs and see the finery' at the local parish church. [35] The 1698 Assembly had unanimously agreed that General Baptists 'may not join in the worship of God with those that are not'. They must 'keep themselves pure in ... separation' and if any 'transgress therein' by attending other churches they must be 'carefully and speedily' admonished and made aware of 'the evil and danger that do attend it'. [36] In 1701 the rival General Association proved itself equally strict on the issue. When some Rainham (Essex) members attended a local Presbyterian service, the matter was reported to the wider fellowship. Offenders of this kind were left in no doubt that their conduct was unacceptable. [37] In the following year the question was raised at the General Assembly as to whether a General Baptist member, characteristically holding the 'six principles' of Hebrews 6, might join in worship 'with a church that is not built upon that foundation'. The vote was 'carried in the negative'.[38] Such decisions served to erect an impenetrable wall around these churches at a time when other Christians had convictions which would have enriched their thinking and, possibly, helped to arrest their decline.

But there is more to the story than quarrelsome meetings, petty rivalries, uncertain theology and restrictive insularity. In the life of any denomination few periods can be entirely dismal. Even within a disheartening context such as has been described, good things were certainly accomplished. In the overall picture of depressed life, it is important not to minimize the achievements. During these difficult years the General Baptist people came to recognise the urgent necessity of both an educated and a financially-supported ministry. The 1702 General Association made plans to establish an academy 'in or about' the city of London and delegates were asked to collect subscriptions for this purpose.[39] Two years later the Kent representatives at the General Assembly expressed concern about the 'sinking and languishing condition' of their churches; it was asked if a fund could be established for ministerial support. They clearly regarded a full-time, paid ministry as a crucial factor in arresting 'the great decay' which was taking place within the ·life of the denomination.[40] Most of the General Baptist ministers earned their living in other employment and could only devote their free time to the service of the churches. In 1709 their London ministers, for example, included a hatter, butcher, ribbon-weaver, tallow-chandler and two tailors, and some General Baptists may have been embarrassed by taunts about their 'mechanic teachers' found in polemical literature like Marius D'Assigny's *The Mystery of Anabaptism Unmasked* .[41] The Assembly of 1704 had asked their ministers to preach on the subject of a full-time, paid ministry in order to remove prejudices that it might not be scriptural. It was suggested that specific people should be appointed in each church to collect monthly subscriptions for this purpose.

Although the churches were familiar with the practice of raising money for the payment of Messengers' expenses, the support of local ministers was a more ambitious venture and there is little evidence that many churches were able to respond positively to the Assembly's decision.

The resolution about the financial support of local ministers is a further illustration of the denomination's connexionalism. Although such money was to be collected

29

within local churches, it was not to stay with them. The total amount was to be despatched periodically to the Assembly's treasurer so that funds could be fairly allocated to those churches where the need was greatest.

There was certainly a fear that collecting money for local ministers might divert funds from the support of the denomination's Messengers. By 1710 the churches were told that more Messengers were urgently needed to give pastoral help to 'those in distressed churches that are ready to languish and perish'. Congregations 'destitute of a fixed ministry' were in a 'very deplorable' condition and, as it was evidently beyond their means to support their own pastor on a full-time basis, it was thought that the shared ministry provided by Messengers might be one way of meeting the need. Churches were asked to organise, wherever possible, the weekly collection of either a farthing or half-penny from each member, to be forwarded to the local association each year, which would in turn send it on to the Assembly.[42]

It is clear that the General Baptists had good reason to be concerned about the ministry. It was not only that many churches were without adequate pastoral oversight; some who had ministers were anxious about their conduct. The 1711 Assembly was troubled that some ministers openly encouraged cock-fighting, dancing and 'many other vices'. Such men were plainly told that behaviour of this kind ought to disqualify the minister from pastoral office 'until he shall appear of another mind and give satisfaction to the church'.[43] General Baptists were plainly worried about the inconsistent life-style of some ministers and their families. The Colchester church had earlier shared its unhappiness about their 'perriwigs and high dresses'; guilty ministers were urged to 'reform themselves and [their] families'. Such expressions of the 'sin of covetousness',[44] as they described it, were not confined to the General Baptists. Hercules Collins (died 1702) and Benjamin Keach voiced similar complaints about the powdered wigs and sartorial habits of London's Particular Baptists at this time.[45]

It is a further commendable feature of General Baptists in this period that, despite their pastoral and doctrinal preoccupations, they took an interest in the promotion of the denomination's work overseas. At the height of the Christological controversy in 1702, members of the General Association received a request from the General Baptists of Carolina. The colonists asked whether their English friends could possibly 'supply them with a ministry or with books'.

Deeply conscious of their own ministerial needs, the Association regretted that at that stage they could not help by supplying men, but they did raise a substantial sum of money to provide literature.[46] Some time prior to 1714 an approach had evidently been made to the General Assembly's churches concerning help for General Baptist work in Virginia. In the Assembly of that year the representatives were urged speedily to return the money collected for the support of Messengers to be sent to America. Once the funds were in hand the appointed Messengers were to travel to Virginia 'with all convenient speed'. The necessary help must have been found because Robert Norden, an elder at Warbleton, Kent, and Thomas White sailed for Virginia in 1714. Only Norden survived the journey and by 1725 he had returned home,[47] though the Assembly of that year gave him full permission to return to Virginia if he wished to do so.[48] It is a pity more is not known about the precise work of these courageous men who settled in the colonies.[49]

The needs of Ireland were frequently discussed by General Baptists in the early eighteenth century but little appears to have been done until 1721, when James Richardson and William Wood were sent there 'to settle the affairs' of the Irish churches. The cost of these journeys was met by the churches in fellowship with the Assembly.[50] Some were slow in supporting the venture: three years later the delegates agreed to send a letter to those congregations, mainly in Essex and Kent, known to be 'deficient in defraying the charge' of supporting these ministers' work in Ireland.[51]

Commendable concern was also expressed by General Baptists in this period for the promotion of Christian education. The instruction of children was believed to be of paramount importance and several catechisms were produced by General Baptist writers. Many were concerned that this excellent material was not being used as widely as it deserved, and the Assembly urged the churches to press home the teaching responsibility entrusted to Christian parents. In 1715 all the churches were told of the 'great neglect in not catechizing' children with the result that 'so many degenerate from the ways of God and so embrace no religion at all'. Family worship appears to have been widely neglected and ministers were asked to preach on such matters. Congregations were exhorted to make full use of 'those useful catechisms written by our faithful brethren which belong to our Communion as seasonable helps to those that need assistance therein'.[52]

Although deflected by marginal issues, some early eighteenth-century General Baptist writers succeeded in making a modest contribution to Christian theology. Their most significant work concerned the doctrine of baptism, and none was more important than that of the London General Baptist preacher, John Gale (1680-1722). Educated at Amsterdam and later at Leiden, where he obtained a doctorate, Gale gave sustained attention to the baptismal debate which followed the publication of William Wall's *History of Infant Baptism* (1705). At this time in his mid-twenties, Gale brought a keen mind to Wall's comprehensive study of the subject and in 1711 produced his *Reflections on Mr Wall's History ... in several letters to a friend*. This substantial work of over 500 pages was a careful response to Wall's ideas and made it clear that it was possible to be a General Baptist and a gifted scholar at the same time. The Presbyterian, James Foster, was baptised as a believer as a consequence of reading it. Foster was to become one of the most well-known preachers among the General Baptists. Later, unlike Gale, he gradually moved away from orthodox theology to a pattern of teaching markedly influenced by the rationalistic thinking of the time.

Although the story is relieved by positive achievements, the early eighteenth-century account of General Baptist life is rarely inspiring. Assembly and Association records constantly refer to their poor spiritual health. Aware of 'careless walking and deadness of spirit and want of love to God and to one another', they confessed 'congregational sins' that are 'against clear light and dear love' (1711).[53] They were distressed about the 'sinking state of religion' (1719)[54] and concerned that in 1728 'the Baptist interest' was still 'so unhappily divided'. Grieved that their Master and Lord, 'the kind, compassionate Jesus', was displeased with them, they pleaded with one another to become 'repairers of the breach'. In an earnest endeavour to create a more evident unity, they repeatedly asked their churches to recognise that some difference of opinion was inevitable; it is unrealistic to expect that they should all be exactly of one mind. They affirmed their common allegiance to the 'six principles' of Hebrews and made this the basis of their union. They knew from painful experience that serious divisions 'must of necessity weaken our hands'.[55] Their corporate penitence and noble resolution were commendable but, as the years went by, their disunity and fragmentation became worse rather than better. The 'clear light' of biblical teaching was gradually becoming obscured, and the 'dear love' of their earlier fellowship a haunting memory. Unless the decline could be quickly arrested, their effective witness would be imperilled.

* * * * * * * *

'Earnest hopes'

We turn now from the General Baptists to their contemporaries in the Calvinistic Baptist churches of England. During the later part of the reign of James II, London's Particular Baptist ministers had occasionally met together to consider the state of the churches throughout the country. The new religious freedom under William and Mary enabled them to call together representatives of congregations from various parts of the land. Three months after the General Baptists had met for their 1689 Assembly, the Particular Baptists did the same. A letter of invitation over the signatures of respected leaders like William Kiffin (1616-1701) and Hanserd Knollys (1599-1691) was despatched to most of the churches known to them which shared their convinced Calvinism and distinctively Baptist churchmanship. The omission of some churches, albeit few, is the first indication that the Particular Baptists were not as closely united as might at first appear. London's Barbican church welcomed both Arminian and Calvinistic Baptists as its members: it was not invited to send representatives to the assembly, nor were those churches with 'Seventh Day' convictions who thought it incumbent on them to worship on Saturdays. Although in a minority, most of these 'Seventh Day' congregations were just as persuaded about Calvinistic theology as those who received the invitation, but the London leaders had no intention of welcoming them to the first national assembly. The deliberate rejection of these churches was ominous; there were divisions in the ranks already and as the decades went by more serious disagreements were to make the continuance of national assemblies virtually impossible.

Structures

One significant characteristic of Particular Baptist life in the late seventeenth century and later was the persistent ambition to act unitedly through a partnership of churches. As we have noted, however, there were things to divide them. Other divisions were on the immediate horizon, yet, for all that, many of these churches were determined not to do their work independently. They were not in the same sense committed to the connexional principle which, from the beginning, had characterised the life of the General Baptists. The autonomy of the local fellowship of believers was an important aspect of Particular Baptist ecclesiology, but that did not commit them to insularity or detachment. Their emphasis on congregational partnership and interdependence is given expression at this time in four specific enterprises: national assemblies, local associations, ministers' fraternals and a ministerial fund. Each of these may be considered in turn.

The first national assembly was held, as planned, in September 1689. It welcomed delegates from over a hundred churches. The letter of invitation[1] recorded the 'earnest hopes and long expectations' which the new reign had encouraged, and representatives came to London seeking not only mutual inspiration but a new sense of direction. They were hardly complacent. Their London correspondents had confessed that in various parts of the country much of their 'former strength, life and vigour' had been dissipated, but a new sense of expectancy was also in the air. It was widely held that the scene could quickly change for the better, especially if the churches could be supplied with full-time ministers. This theme of adequately supported and well-educated pastoral oversight was to dominate the assembly and eventually alienate some of its members.

The 1689 Assembly met for ten days, giving itself to serious discussion and emerged with several practical suggestions covering a wide range of topics.[2] There was a commendable evangelistic impulse. A ministry with appropriate financial support might be free to devote its energies to 'the great work of preaching the gospel' and men might be sent both 'where the gospel has or has not yet been preached'. There was strong pastoral motivation. Specific disciplinary matters were openly shared, including the question of mixed marriages. On this issue Particular Baptists were more flexible than the General Baptist leaders. Believers were to marry 'in the Lord', but there was no attempt whatever to interpret the phrase restrictively by limiting it to those who belonged only to the fellowship of the 'baptized churches'. There was a declared educational programme. Those who believed themselves called to the ministry were to be helped to attain 'the knowledge and understanding of the languages, Latin, Greek and Hebrew' and such young men were to be commended to an appointed group of nine London ministers 'by any two of the churches that belong to this assembly'. The fact that two churches were required to support a candidate for the ministry is an informative comment on their interdependent ecclesiology. Those prospective ministers who 'are disposed for study' and 'have an inviting gift' must have their call tested by believers of a congregation other than the one where they are best known. Unlike the General Baptists, the discussions even had a modest ecumenical perspective. The question was asked whether members of their churches were 'at liberty to hear any sober and pious men of the Independent and Presbyterian persuasions, when they had no opportunity to attend upon the preaching of the word in their own assembly, or had no other to preach unto them'. The biblical reference cited by way of authority for listening to other preachers (Acts 18.24-26) was slightly condescending, but they were at least free to worship elsewhere if necessity demanded it, which was more than the General Baptists were allowed to do. The local Independent or Presbyterian 'Apollos' might have needed to know 'the way of God more perfectly', but Particular Baptists saw that there was no harm in taking advantage of the ministry of any 'eloquent man' who was 'mighty in the scriptures'. But the ecumenism did not extend to 'the national church'. Those who forsook their local congregation of baptized believers for worship at the parish church were to be reclaimed, wherever possible, but, if not responsive to admonition, ejected. Moreover, there was a predominant doctrinal concern in the meetings. Members agreed to republish the 1677 Confession. Questions about Calvinistic theology and its practical interpretation found their way on to the agenda. The enquiry as to whether their members were 'not actually reconciled to God, actually justified, and adopted' on the day when Christ died was the harbinger of later divisive controversies within the churches when points of serious dispute arose over abstruse aspects of the doctrine of salvation. The 1689 representatives were firmly told that believers cannot possibly be 'actually reconciled, justified, or adopted, until they are really implanted into Jesus Christ by faith' for 'the Scripture attributes all these benefits to faith as the instrumental cause of them'. The question is deeply significant: it indicates that highly controversial issues concerning predestination and election were already under debate in the churches. The answer to the question may well have satisfied those who asked it in 1689; thirty or forty years later it would have initiated interminable controversy. Although its discussions moved freely over a variety of different subjects of common concern, the Assembly led its delegates conclusively to an urgent financial obligation. The full-time ministry had the most prominent place in their conversations and they resolved they should do something practical to meet that declared need. A fund was to be established and the money collected in the churches sent to one of nine London ministers 'appointed to receive it'.

The Assembly was to be the first of four, held each year from 1689 to 1692. Three things need to be said about these assemblies. First, they were dominated by London. In one sense, that was their strength. Without the initiative of a closely-knit group of ministers, the assemblies might never have been convened. But there is good evidence that London's ministerial ideals were not held with equal vigour throughout the country. In particular, as we shall see, the necessity, or even importance, of classical languages as part of ministerial education, in order that 'they may be capable of defending the truth against opposers', was vigorously challenged. It may have been an administrative necessity for the ministerial fund collections to be sent to London, just as it may have been expedient for the appointed London ministers to interview ministerial candidates, but this may well have served to create the impression of dominance by a metropolitan elite. Within a few years this slightly top-heavy leadership structure was to lose its national identity altogether.

The second consideration about the national assembly pattern is that it was preoccupied with ministry. London's Particular Baptist pastors had doubtless felt more than a little uneasy when, on numerous occasions, they were unfavourably contrasted intellectually with their fellow-dissenters. The years of persecution had thrust them alongside colleagues in the Presbyterian and Independent ministry. They had stood before magistrates in the same courts and spent time in the same prisons. They had come to recognise that many of these colleagues in the ministry were better educated and, now that the persecution was over, most of them naturally hoped to be more adequately supported financially. Baptist ministers had been exposed to ridicule and summarily dismissed as ignorant tallow-chandlers or uneducated butchers. Presbyterians and Independents united in 1690[3] to establish a Common Fund for the education and support of the ministry and Baptists were eager to do the same. The combined accusation of ignorance and engagement in secular work was to be a sore point with Particular Baptist ministers for several years. David Russen's hostile *Fundamentals Without a Foundation* (1702)[4] drew attention to their daily employment. On an August Saturday in 1715 the Tory newspaper, *The Weekly Journal,* named some London Baptist ministers who 'were all formerly of very mean occupations'. One of them, Nathaniel Hodges (1675-1727), was sarcastically congratulated that his former trade had obviously helped him in 'the curing of souls', a pun on the work of a shoemaker. The fact that both Benjamin Stinton and Thomas Crosby went to considerable lengths to answer these charges and comment that Jewish rabbis also engaged in secular occupations, that the disciples were honest fishermen, Luke a physician, Paul a tent-maker, and, most of all, Christ a carpenter, shows how sensitive the matter continued to be within the life of Baptist churches. [5] The 1689 Assembly and those which met over the next few years continued to devote a fair amount of their time to the issue of ministerial education and support. The London ministers may even have looked enviously at the authority of the minister within Presbyterianism as well as at the better education which had shared in the making of many Independent ministers. Some of the later controversies which disturbed the life of London churches over hymn-singing were not simply about worship. In several cases they were related to undercurrents about ministerial authority.

We have just hinted at a third characteristic of national assemblies: they were beset by controversy. The 1692 Assembly recognised that one particular topic had become the occasion of 'uncharitable, unsavoury censures, reflections, and reproaches'. The ranks of the Particular Baptists had become seriously divided over hymn-singing. Strong views had been expressed on both sides. A prolonged pamphlet war had maintained the tension and the controversy assumed serious proportions. The delegates were troubled, it seems, not so much over the propriety of hymns as about the inappropriate language used by contestants on both sides. A small committee was appointed to examine the relevant writings. It came to the conclusion that offensive books or pamphlets on the subject should be called in, and church members urged not to 'buy, give or disperse' any such books as have 'uncharitable reflections in them against their brethren'. We shall have to return to the hymn-singing controversy later. At this point it is sufficient to observe that the dissension it caused within the ranks of London Particular Baptists alone was probably one factor in bringing their pattern of annual national assemblies to an abrupt end.

In 1692 it was thought best to divide the Particular Baptist churches into two main groupings. In each year one 'Assembly' would meet in London, the other in Bristol, the second largest city in the country. The Bristol meetings were to be held at Easter, followed by those in London at Whitsun. The London and Bristol assemblies would each send two representatives to one another's meetings and each would produce an annual printed account of their deliberations. The one planned for the west of England maintained a vigorous and effective life and continued to be known as 'the Western Association'. The London assembly was doomed to failure. The painful divisions we have just noted made any exercise in partnership highly precarious. In 1693 the Bristol delegates gave expression to their underlying discontent about the place of classical and biblical languages in ministerial education. In order to 'remove all jealousies' and misunderstandings, they declared that it was not the 'intention or design' of their assembly 'in relation to the education of youth, to promote human learning ... or to make them equal with the gifts of the Spirit'. In forceful language they unanimously affirmed that they 'abhor such a principle and practice, being satisfied and assured, that the gift for edification is a distinct thing from acquired parts, and that men may attain the greatest degrees in human learning, and yet notwithstanding be ignorant of Christ, and his glorious gospel'. They affirmed that 'God does sometimes bestow greater gifts ... on some who have not attained the knowledge of the tongues, than he does on some others who have; ... That they greatly abuse their knowledge of the tongues, who are puffed up thereby to lean upon it, and to despise their brethren, who have the gift for edification, though they have not the same acquired abilities. That the knowledge of the tongues is not in itself essential, or absolutely necessary to constitute a minister of the gospel; ... Dare we to limit the Holy One, who bestows the gift for edification upon the learned, as well as the unlearned, and who chooses some of the wise, prudent, learned, though not many'. [6]

Six weeks after that assembly, Andrew Gifford, Snr (1642-1721), and George Fownes were sent to London as Bristol's appointed representatives. They must have been aware of differing views on the education of ministers. London had emphasised the importance of learning, Bristol the necessity of gift. Continuing controversy within the London churches meant that within a year or two the London meetings were no longer held. Only Bristol continued its meetings and as early as 1694 sent a letter to William Kiffin and William Collins for communication to the London delegates at their Whitsun meetings. It told them that 'they were grieved because' the London leaders 'who some few years ago did zealously promote such associations for the general good of the churches and the glory of Christ, have declined it'. They complained, 'You know how often the country sent to London, whilst you have sent but once to the country, and are weary'. [7]

Association meetings had long played a significant part in the life of the Particular Baptists. Now that the days of partial toleration had arrived, regional gatherings of local church representatives were recommenced in several parts of the country. Minutes and circulars from the Abingdon, Midland, Northern and Western Associations for the opening decades of the eighteenth century present a lively picture of work in the churches. The procedure was much the same wherever the meetings were held. The local church was normally represented by its minister and one other member who brought to the association a letter, carefully composed by their church, describing its life, problems, encouragements and ambitions. The meetings were spread over two or three days and always devoted time to preaching and mutual exhortation as well as discussion. The programme was arranged so that queries raised by the churches concerning pastoral or doctrinal matters could be debated and the churches informed of the association's common mind. At the close of the meetings a circular letter was prepared over the signature of the presiding minister or moderator and sent to all the associated churches.

The range of issues discussed by associations provides an interesting insight into matters of importance to the participating congregations. In 1695 the Yorkshire and Lancashire delegates were asked to express their mind about the assumption of superiority by David Crosley (1669-1744) over some northern churches on the ground that the Bromsgrove church had ordained him as a travelling evangelist; the churches were told that the association did not accept Crosley's oversight nor recognise the authenticity of such roving commissions. [8] When the Berkshire Association met in 1708 it discussed the need to encourage young men to consider the possibility that God might be calling them to the ministry, and practical discussion followed about the best ways of equipping them for such service. Their Circular Letter for that year is not restricted to local ecclesiastical concerns. It looks out on the wider world and mentions the country's war with France, as well as the low moral condition of England. [9]

In 1704 an attempt was made to encourage inter-church relationships between the Particular Baptists of London and the Home Counties. In that year thirteen churches were eager to discuss aspects of their common life and work, but divisive factors were still present. Some churches objected strongly to the presence of the Barbican church in view of its willingness to receive both Calvinists and Arminians into its fellowship. The inclusion of the Pinners' Hall church, with its Seventh Day convictions, was a stumbling-block to others. Five churches withdrew and within two or three years this newly-revived Association had ceased to function. However, other opportunities in London for the mutual exchange of advice and counsel were to take its place.

One of these was the ministers' fraternal, though in this period it was not known by that name. We have already seen that several London pastors appear to have been sensitive about their ministerial status. Various meetings brought them into direct contact with Presbyterian and Independent colleagues; in March 1702, for example, ministers from the Three Denominations combined to present an Address to the Throne.[10] Contacts with leaders in other denominations may have served to heighten their sense of ministerial responsibility, privilege and dignity. By 1714 onwards Baptist ministers in London were meeting weekly at the Hanover Coffee-House in Finch Lane. This was an unusual fraternal, providing a rare opportunity for both General and Particular Baptist ministers to talk together.[11] However, with the increasing fear of Arianism and Socinianism,[12] which followed the Salters' Hall controversy, a number of Particular Baptists became strongly opposed to fraternising with General Baptists and in January 1723/24 another fraternal was formed which denied access to any but convinced Calvinists. This theologically exclusive meeting became known as the Baptist Board. Its early records are a fascinating study of ministerial priorities in this period. Although initially a small group, the Board's influence extended far beyond London and its advice was sought by many provincial ministers in need of guidance and advice. One minister wrote from Dublin asking whether his London colleagues thought it right for him to go to South Carolina. Others sought help on moral and ethical questions. A deputation came to the Board asking whether their church ought to erect a new meeting-house. Counsel was naturally sought about disciplinary issues within churches. Ministers invited their colleagues to say whether they thought it fitting for them to respond positively to an invitation to a different pastorate. Churches equally sought the Board's help when they were looking for a new minister.[13] It is important to see that, in the case of these London ministers, the Board tended to take over some of the work which in other parts of the country properly belonged to the local association. The limitation to ministers, however, was a London peculiarity and was not copied in the provinces.

41

Another highly influential feature of Baptist life at this time was the formation in 1717 of the Particular Baptist Fund. Its aim was to provide educational resources for prospective ministers and help for the support of poorly-paid men already engaged in pastoral ministry. The Fund's managers were committed to Calvinistic theology and determined to keep General Baptists away from its work, either as donors or beneficiaries. Its emergence may represent not only the dominance of Calvinistic theology, but an understandable desire on the part of the London Particular Baptist laity to be actively involved in inter-church affairs. Crosby was convinced that the meeting of Baptist leaders at the Hanover Coffee-House had not continued because they had restricted the meeting to ministers; they ought to have included 'one or two from each of their churches of the most prudent and moderate of their laity'.[14] Some laymen had asked why a Loyal Address had to be presented by ministers only. There was clearly a feeling that the London churches were in danger of clerical domination. It is important to understand that the fund was far more than a money-raising enterprise. Its managers were not only impeccably orthodox but highly influential. It was also a partnership of churches and not simply the benevolent preoccupation of individuals. In many respects it was by this means that the ideals of the 1689-92 assemblies were put into practice. For some time the earlier resolutions had been left as a series of pious hopes, but now, at last, the money was being raised.

Furthermore, the fund was prompted by a genuine concern about the breakdown in partnership between the Particular Baptist churches of England. Its initial letter to the churches 'in and about' London commented on the initiators' 'great grief and trouble' at the 'little correspondence and union there is' between the churches of the 'denomination', as well as the serious shortage of ministers and the abject poverty of the few that there were. The proposal was that every church that could advance '£50 or upwards' would be entitled to send one Messenger with their minister. Each additional £50 entitled them to a further Messenger and it would be the responsibility of these representatives to serve as managers. Six London congregations combined to establish the fund and, in the summer of 1717, its excellent work began.[15] It was used to raise the level of ministerial support and constantly pressed home the claims of an adequate salary-structure from a biblical point of view. It kept a careful eye on local church giving, generous or otherwise; in their communications the managers made it abundantly clear that they had no intention of offering aid to mean churches. The case of one minister 'was presented and rejected because of the ability and neglect of his church'. Its early records show that it was used as an agency of compassionate help in cases of distressing family need:

> Agreed that the money given to Mr Wright before his decease be paid to the wife in consideration of a great family of children.

> It was reported that Mr Thomas of Waly was dead, and moved [that] the money allowed him might be paid to his daughter in consideration of her care and the great charge she had been at with her father.

The managers were theologically alert as well as practically concerned. An application in respect of one minister was 'presented and rejected upon some information he had changed his principles', but in a later letter the man concerned 'vindicated himself touching his principles' and the award was agreed. [16]

The year after the establishment of the fund, a grant was made to John Gill (1697-1771) of Kettering, a candidate for the ministry in his early twenties. Gill was a gifted Hebraist and never forgot the help he had received from the fund to support him during a period of fruitful study and early pastoral experience. He was later to come to London as one of the denomination's most outstanding preachers and writers as well as a manager, for almost fifty years, of the Particular Baptist Fund. The generosity shown to the young Gill is a reminder that the managers were concerned with the work of 'educating young men for the Ministry'. Applicants for assistance of this kind were to appear before a small group of managers who might 'be the better able to judge of the person's capacity to receive education' and decide 'what sort of assistance to give him'. Their first grants were made for the purchase of essential books. Gill bought Hebrew texts with the £17 allocated to him. It was agreed that no young man who was being helped in this way must in any circumstances 'decline or neglect the frequent exercise of his ministerial gifts' during his studies. The managers recognised that study and gift are inseparable partners. Neither was it thought necessary to encourage these young men to abandon their secular employment during their period of study. A trainee-minister was not 'obliged to lay down or quit his secular calling... while he is perfecting his studies by the encouragement and assistance of this fund'.[17]

There were even occasions when the fund was able to exercise a pastoral function. When John Gill came to be minister in London, the inviting church suffered a division, ostensibly because women's votes had been counted in his favour when it had not been the church's practice to include them. Gill eventually took his supporters off to form another church, but the fund was later able to exercise a reconciling ministry between the two congregations so that both of them came to participate in the administration of the fund.[18] The division may not have been occasioned simply by voting procedures; it is likely that some of the members had been happier with the moderate Calvinism of their former minister, Benjamin Stinton, and had hoped for a similar man to replace him. Gill represented high Calvinism and the continuing discussion of such views hardly promoted denominational unity within the life of the Particular Baptist people. It will be necessary to return to this important topic.

Controversies

Since the late seventeenth century, three divisive issues had begun to assume prominence in the churches. They concerned the imposition of hands at baptism, the 'Seventh Day' observance of 'the Christian Sabbath' and the practice of congregational hymn-singing.

We have already seen that General Baptists were persuaded that the laying on of hands ought to accompany the baptism of every believer. Keach continued to maintain this position even after he joined the Particular Baptists, and he was not a solitary voice within his new environment. The controversy had a long history. When, in 1674, Henry Danvers republished his fiercely-criticised work on baptism, he was at pains to repudiate the practice of imposition of hands.[19] In the following year Keach produced a pamphlet, published anonymously under the title *Darkness Vanquished, or Faith in its primitive purity*. In this work he defended the practice and it is clear that he continued to maintain these views among Particular Baptists. In 1698 his original pamphlet was enlarged and published in his name as *Laying on of Hands upon Baptized Believers, as such, proved an ordinance of Christ*. In this work Keach maintained that through this ordinance the believer can 'meet with more of Christ and his Spirit'. He was persuaded that the laying on of hands is not the means whereby the Spirit is imparted initially; he recognised that a believer cannot exercise faith

44

until the Spirit is actively at work within him. He did believe, however, that the imposition of hands is a confirmatory rite; it strengthens the assurance of faith:

> 'tis the great benefit received and enjoyed by believers to be sealed by the Spirit: 'tis not a matter of rejoicing to work miracles, as 'tis to know our names are written in heaven. [20]

It seems that Keach held these views so strongly that he was unwilling to welcome into the membership of his church any but those whose baptism had been accompanied by the imposition of hands, but in this restriction he was not widely followed.

The practice continued among churches other than Keach's. Strong views on the matter troubled the Wapping church in the early eighteenth century. [21] David Rees (1683-1748) and his Limehouse congregation were committed to it, [22] but gradually the practice began to die out amongst the Particular Baptists. Two women who transferred to John Gill's London church in 1721 felt obliged to submit to it 'having not at their first entrance into the Christian Church come under the ordinance of laying on of hands, it being not the practice of those churches to which they gave up themselves', but were willing to 'submit thereunto and had hands laid on them according to the practice and example of the holy apostles'. By 1729 Gill had moved in his thinking on the subject and was becoming uneasy about its practice. The church agreed that, as he had declared 'his dissatisfaction in using the custom of laying on of hands at the admission of members', he was to be 'left at his liberty in the point for the future'. [23] Although the topic had given rise to some heated discussion at the turn of the century, it did not create serious division among Particular Baptists, though it continued to trouble General Baptist churches in some places until the late eighteenth century. Among English Calvinistic Baptists the practice ceased to feature either in baptismal services or at the reception of new members; in course of time it virtually disappeared from their worship.

Keach was not only an apologist for the imposition of hands, he was also an opponent of 'Seventh Day' Baptists. [24] We have seen that the popular London preacher, Joseph Stennett, held these views, though they did not prevent him from enjoying contacts with his fellow Particular Baptists. Together with his congregation he kept Saturday as the Christian sabbath, and used that day for conducting worship among the 'Seventh Day' churches. Stennett had been used to this custom from childhood. His father, the physician-preacher Edward Stennett (died 1691), had written pamphlets advocating such views during the persecution period and had conducted a steady discussion by correspondence with Baptists in America on Sabbatarian ideas. A significant number of 'Seventh Day' churches existed in England at the turn of the century, three of them in London. Stennett regularly preached for his Particular Baptist friends on Sundays as well as for his own congregation on Saturdays. His London ministry extended from 1690 until his death in 1713. The fact that Stennett's sabbatarianism was opposed by Edward Elliott, the Wapping Particular Baptist minister, shows that these views were far from dead in the early eighteenth century.

This literal interpretation of Old Testament teaching about the sabbath was a threat to some Particular Baptist leaders and an unremitting pamphlet war extended from the persecution period onwards, enlisting among the opponents of the view such writers as John Bunyan (1628-88), Isaac Marlow (1649-1719) and Benjamin Keach. Some General Baptists were won over to 'Seventh Day' views, like John Maulden (1644-1714), who published the reasons for his change of mind about the right day for Christian worship. Keach was to the forefront in this controversy, as with other divisive issues in the period. In 1700 he published his forthright *Jewish Sabbath abrogated ... wherein are many new arguments not found in former authors,* and his book is but one among many. A preacher like Joseph Stennett could retain close friendships with men and women who did not subscribe to his sabbatarian teaching but, encouraged by an incessant supply of polemical literature, lesser men were in danger of becoming quarrelsome and hostile in such discussions. In an already divided community, the 'Seventh Day' question was yet another contentious topic.

We have already mentioned the names of Isaac Marlow and Benjamin Keach. They were united in their opposition to the 'Seventh Day' people, but ferocious and bitter opponents in the hymn-singing controversy. Marlow was a reasonably prosperous London jeweller, Keach a hard-working minister who had to keep a bookshop to supplement his income. As the controversy unfolds it is clear that they were not simply arguing about hymns, however deeply they may have felt about the subject. The debate exposed submerged resentment. Marlow, the layman, objected strongly to the ministerial dominance of which Keach was possibly a conspicuous example.

Keach had hoped that the topic might have been discussed at the 1689 Assembly, but its leaders feared that such a course might prove disruptive. Marlow, an influential layman and the Assembly's treasurer, was fiercely opposed to hymn-singing, which was still a novelty, and devoted his considerable ability to exposing its dangers. With a variety of arguments the anti-singing lobby fervently complained against such 'false worship'.[25] They maintained that there was little difference between the 'error' of singing hymns, 'made in artificial rhymes', and using set prayers, that such compositions could only, at best, reflect the experience of the writer and to sing them publicly might put lies into the mouths of others, and that the practice would encourage unbelievers to use words which were not matched by genuine, personal faith.[26] The use of 'rhymes in a set form' as part of corporate worship was summarily dismissed by one writer as 'a mere human invention of ballad singing'.[27] On both sides, meticulous expositions began to deteriorate into vitriolic attacks. At one point Marlow listed some of the abusive terms which had been used to describe him: he had been called a 'ridiculous scribbler' with a 'brazen-forehead',[28] but his opponents had no monopoly of abusive language. Marlow and his colleagues were equally discourteous. The controversy went on and London Particular Baptists became bitterly divided. Keach had weight, Marlow had money. Moreover, the older statesmen of the denomination often found themselves on opposite sides of the debate. After years of unbroken harmony, Hanserd Knollys favoured singing and William Kiffin opposed it, and their differences appeared in print. It was yet another issue which seriously disturbed the relationships between these London churches at a time when they might have been offering creative leadership to their colleagues in the rest of the country.

In time, the storm settled down. Ultimately defeated, Marlow left London for Leominster but, significantly, devoted his closing years to the study of church order. He worked carefully on a manuscript which was meant to form the second part of his *The Purity of Gospel Communion* (1694). If Marlow's teaching is compared with that of Keach's *The Glory of a true church* (1697), it becomes apparent that it was not only the singing issue which kept the two men apart. Neither Keach nor his son, Elias, had time for interfering lay busy-bodies, comparing them with those in Old Testament times who 'meddled with the priest's work and office'.[29] Marlow considered that ministerial autocrats were dangerous manipulators who must constantly be resisted. Keach may well have exaggerated the role of the minister but, at the time, his emphasis may have been necessary. For too long the churches had been without a well-educated or adequately supported ministry.

Achievements

The new era was marked by three significant denominational achievements - increasing concern to provide for the training and support of the ministry, pioneer work in children's education, and some modest ventures in ecumenical partnership.

Keach had taken a leading part in the campaign for a new pattern for ministerial training and maintenance. It was not simply a case of raising money for the ministers' salaries. The wider topic of the importance, influence and role of the minister was given constant attention in the opening decades of this period.

It was recognised that the regular supply of ministers must always be in the mind of the churches. The 1689 Assembly reminded the Particular Baptist people that the 'inviting gift' must certainly be encouraged.[30] The local church had a responsibility before God to discern which young men among its members might be equipped for the full-time ministry. John Piggott told his contemporaries that they 'must not expect that preachers will drop down from heaven, or spring out of [the] earth; but due care must be taken for the encouragement of humble men that have *real gifts,* and let such be trained up in *useful learning,* that they may be able to defend the truths they preach'.[31] Hercules Collins expressed his concern in 1702 that 'so little provision' is 'made in the churches of Christ for a future ministry'. The congregations are 'the schools of Christ' and they must look around their young members 'to see what spiritual gifts God has given them' and be determined to 'put them into their proper exercise'.[32]

Training was another important issue. Piggott was supporting the earlier resolutions of the 1689 Assembly when he reminded the Particular Baptists of his day that 'useful learning' must not be neglected. We have already noted the Bristol Assembly's cautionary word about the place of classical and biblical languages as an essential part of that training, but few of the London ministers had any doubt

48

about the importance of a good educational foundation. Hercules Collins made the practical suggestion that the elders in the churches should 'set apart some time every week for the instructing [of] young men... inclined to divine studies' and that small churches in the country should join together in order to have a similar training group which 'would agree to meet once a month, or more often, to hear the gifts that God has given their churches'.[33] He pressed home the necessity of diligent study and wide reading, not in order 'to get men's *hums* and applause by quaint and eloquent speech, but above all to please God, and win souls'.[34] He does not exalt human learning, but neither will he allow it to be deprecated. In the early eighteenth century practical steps were taken to see that suitably gifted young men were provided with the intellectual help they needed. Some candidates for the ministry were trained by senior ministers who took them into their homes for this purpose. Joseph Stennett did this in later life so that prospective young ministers might have 'direction in their studies'.[35] Earlier, the young Plymouth member, Richard Sampson, had been tutored by William Thomas in Bristol. Edmund Calamy tells us that Thomas (not a Baptist) 'trained up many for the Ministry'.[36] What is of special interest to us is that Sampson's fees and maintenance at Thomas's home were met by the new fund set up by the 1689 Assembly. When the Plymouth church made its initial contribution of £27 and promised a further annual sum of £9, it stipulated that the money be devoted entirely to ministerial training.[37]

The best known of all training schemes in this period is that which began with the initiative of the Bristol elder, Edward Terrill (1635-86).[38] In the persecution period, when many of his contemporaries would have predicted that there was no future for Dissent, Terrill made provision in his will for the education of young ministers. In 1679 Terrill signed a deed of gift which would enable the Broadmead church to support a minister 'well skilled' in biblical languages who would equip young men for their life's ministry. By 1720 Terrill's dream became a reality. In that year Bernard Foskett (1685-1758) was appointed by the Broadmead church for this purpose. His first two students were Welshmen whose financial needs were met not only by Terrill's legacy but also by grants from the Particular Baptist Fund and the Bristol Baptist Fund which had also been established in 1717. Thus was begun the work of the academy at Bristol which was to have so great an influence.[39]

Young men in training had to be supported; so had older

men in churches not in a position to meet the cost of an adequate stipend. Most ministers at the turn of the century were seriously underpaid, even those with a fine reputation. Joseph Stennett's biographer says he had 'a large family, and little to support it'.[40] The maintenance of the ministry was a topic to which the Particular Baptists of the period constantly and of necessity returned. Keach had served them well by producing his important book, *The Gospel Minister's Maintenance Vindicated*. It appeared in the year prior to the 1689 Assembly and its preface indicated that the views it expounded were not those of the author alone. Hanserd Knollys, William Kiffin and Richard Adams (died 1719) had identified themselves with Keach in this earnest appeal to 'the congregations of baptized believers in England and Wales'. Rejoicing that the new reign had given these churches 'respite' from their 'former sufferings',[41] it expressed concern that those cruel years had witnessed the removal of 'so many able and pious men'.[42] There was little hope of replacing them unless the churches would face the responsibility of financing the full-time work of well-equipped successors. Some men in the ministry were lying 'under unsupportable burdens'.[43] Keach pressed for high standards. The men appointed must be people of quality who could earn an adequate salary in other employment. Must they be in poverty because they are 'devoted to a better service'?[44] Keach used scripture, reason and wit to put his message across. He knew of some who argued that ministers should not be paid; they ought not to need financial support. He invited such readers to try the argument on their own employees:

> So perhaps some of your harvest-men that reap down your fields ... can live without their hire and just due etc. yet will that be a good plea (think you) to seek ways or means to with-hold their wages from them?[45]

Keach knew that if a man was to exercise an effective ministry, there was more to it than Sunday preaching. He was meeting the perennial objections of those who ask why it is necessary to pay a man a week's wages for delivering two sermons on Sunday. Perhaps unconsciously echoing the convictions of a writer he suspected, Richard Baxter,[46] Keach insisted that Sunday preaching is 'the least part of his work'. What is the use of the two sermons 'if his matter be not so well-prepared and digested' and how can that be done but by 'careful and diligent study'? And however can 'such poor men ... do this, who are forced to follow their trades hard every day in the week, to get bread for their families'? Moreover, the churches need pastors as well as preachers, for, 'besides the great work of giving themselves up to reading ... and preaching', there is 'another great duty ... which is visiting the members of the church ... Where the work of visiting is neglected, we conclude one main part of the pastor's business lies undone'.[47]

He reminded his readers that pagans freely gave their money to beautify their idols even 'though they impoverished themselves' and 'as for the papists, you cannot be ignorant of what vast treasure they have ... freely bestowed on their Church'.[48]

There is an evangelistic concern which is also part of Keach's appeal. If the small church objects that its tiny congregation cannot possibly demand a week's work from anyone, he asks:

> But do not the neighbouring villages and places adjacent want the Gospel, having no bread for their souls?

Because of this serious neglect,

> the glorious gospel is no more promulgated up and down in dark and blind corners of this nation ... [and] many poor sinners daily perish hereby for want of knowledge'.[49]

The 1689 Assembly invited its churches to study Keach's book and when the Particular Baptist Fund came into being in 1717, his apologia for a full-time, properly supported ministry was once again commended to the churches. Nor was Keach a solitary voice on the subject. David Rees, the Limehouse minister, wrote his *Modest Plea for the Maintenance of the Christian Ministry* in 1722. The churches needed more than one reminder of this important theme.

Another significant Baptist contribution to early eighteenth century education was the establishment of day schools and academies. Several ministers maintained themselves by teaching a few children and from such modest beginnings a number of schools were formed. Joseph Stennett taught for five years before entering the ministry[50] and John Piggott kept a school whilst he was in membership at Goodman's Fields. In the West Country, Ebenezer Wilson of Walbrooke (about 1705) maintained a school at Bristol. Martin Dunsford did the same at Kingsbridge, Devon, whilst he was minister there from 1703-13, as did John Sampson at Tiverton (1714-37).[51]

The denomination's first historian, Thomas Crosby, also had a school in Horsleydown where, from about 1709, he taught arithmetic, algebra, geometry, navigation, astronomy, as well as the 'use of globes, charts and other mathematical instruments and book-keeping'.[52] In 1710 John Ward (1679-1758) opened a school just north of the Thames in Moorfields, which provided a good education 'managed with authority rather than severity' for numerous boys, some of whom became Baptist preachers.[53]

Nonconformists at this time were convinced that children who received free education at Anglican schools were not only catechized but prejudiced against dissenters. One modest attempt at neutralising polemical activity of this kind was to open Nonconformist schools, such as the Charity School established in 1715, also in Horsleydown. Baptists shared with other dissenters in this venture which provided an education for forty boys whose parents were not able to meet the cost of their schooling. The boys were taught, clothed, supplied with Bibles, catechisms (the 1689 Confession with the 96th Article on Baptism removed as an accommodation to the paedobaptist supporters), necessary reading and writing books, as well as 'convenient firing' for Southwark's cold winter days. A Baptist was appointed as its first teacher, Robert Morgan, a member of Stinton's church, and in order to meet the school's expenses the gifts of regular subscribers were supplemented by amounts collected at special sermons preached annually by London dissenting ministers to promote this ecumenical venture in education and social concern.[54]

One more achievement is worthy of note. We have seen that the concern for the ministry, expressed by the Particular Baptist leaders of 1689 and later, may owe something to their earlier contacts during the persecution period with ministers of other denominations. Hard trials had thrown them together, and years in prison had provided many of them with ample time to discuss the problems of their churches. Common sufferings had served to minimise their ecclesiastical differences. When the troubles were over, Keach was not the only minister to remind his fellow-Baptists of the importance of loving other Christians with 'that catholic love that should run in all the veins of everyone that is born of God'.[55] The opening of the eighteenth century certainly gave London Baptists the opportunity to unite with fellow-dissenters, particularly in the quest for religious liberty. The heady exhilaration and relief, which characterised their life under William and Mary, was abruptly followed by some renewed tension and threatened persecution under Anne, the last of the Stuart sovereigns. The Queen's Tory ministers did not favour the toleration of nonconformity and the preaching of hostile Anglican clergy was used to incite mob opposition to dissenters in various parts of the country. Dissenting academies were exercising an increasing influence and the High Church members of the Tory party were angrily concerned. In 1709, Henry Sacheverell preached an inflammatory sermon, later published as *The Perils of False Brethren both in Church and State*. Its wide circulation of 40,000 copies propagated some highly critical views about the academies and in the months that followed some ugly scenes of mob violence resulted in considerable damage to nonconformist meeting-houses, Baptist places of worship being among them.[56] In 1717 twenty-eight dissenting churches and some individuals in eight counties received compensation for damage to property.[57] Attacks of this kind recurred in various parts of the country later in the century.[58]

Dissenters realised that, in the face of continuing opposition to their freedom, it was important for them to act together in the defence of religious liberty. The opening years of the new century witnessed a harsh attack by Tories on the provisions of 'Occasional Conformity'. This practice allowed a dissenter to hold public office by receiving the sacrament prior to election.[59] Generally speaking, Baptists were opposed to this compromise, but some of their fellow dissenters were ready to practise it in order to take part in public affairs. Throughout Anne's reign repeated attempts were made to pass an Occasional Conformity Bill which would make the practice illegal and in that way exclude nonconformists from all positions of responsibility in national life. In 1711 the bill was passed and, following the efforts of Sacheverell and others, was succeeded in 1714 by a Schism Act. This was aimed directly at the academies and schools managed by dissenters and would have seriously limited their increasing influence in the world of education. But Anne died on the very day the Act was to become law and nonconformists widely regarded her passing as a merciful deliverance.

In the face of these strenuous efforts by their opponents, dissenters united for common action. Baptists came alongside their fellow Christians in other dissenting churches. In 1727,

London ministers revived a practice commenced in 1702 of presenting a Loyal Address and joined together for meetings of the General Body of the Three Denominations.[60] Presbyterians and Independents had previously shared in joint ventures, but this was the first time they were formally united with Baptists. Five years later, London ministers were joined by lay members of Presbyterian, Independent and Baptist churches in 1732 for the first meeting of the Protestant Dissenting Deputies.[61] Both these organisations kept a vigilant eye on parliamentary legislation. Although based in London, these two groups acted on behalf of dissenters throughout the country. It was inevitable that, sharing these common concerns, and understandably anxious lest their work should again be restricted by oppressive laws, the dissenters found opportunities to work together. These were ventures in modest but necessary ecumenical co-operation. In this respect, at least, John Piggott's 1704 sermon about Christian unity was being applied to an immediate need: 'It is union and order that render men capable of making a vigorous defence, and that raise them above the fears of an enemy'.[62] Earlier, Richard Allen had told his fellow Baptists that even though they may have 'different apprehensions about more disputable matters of religion',[63] believers must do all within their power to work harmoniously together in co-operative enterprise. Their united activities to guard and extend their freedom were a small but significant beginning in inter-denominational partnership.

* * * * * * * * *

TENSIONS   1730 – 1770

4

'Our unity quite broken'

We must return now to the story of General Baptist congregations. For all dissenters, the early 1730s witnessed an introspective preoccupation with self-assessment. The appearance of numerous pamphlets on 'the present state of the dissenting interest' demanded that nonconformists examine their life and work; various authors offered different explanations for the declining influence of the dissenting churches. Before the appearance of the first of these attempts at nonconformist self-analysis, a Lincolnshire General Baptist minister, largely indifferent to what was happening in other denominations, expressed deep concern about the life of the churches he knew best. John Hursthouse's *Epistle to the baptized churches in Lincolnshire* (1729) did not merely describe the poor spiritual condition of the General Baptists in one county; it voiced a concern which could easily have been expressed by General Baptists in other parts of southern England. He wrote with regret about the 'late contentions' in which they had lost many of their 'best men'. He maintained that denominational affairs had been dictated by 'party interest' and that 'our unity quite broken ... anarchy and disorder' had been 'let in like a flood'. Hursthouse grieves over their 'sinful quarrels' as well as 'the sad decay and the declining state' of the Lincolnshire churches. Painfully aware of the virtual disappearance of 'once flourishing congregations', he is distressed that the majority of General Baptists seem totally unconcerned.[1]

The Lincolnshire Messenger, Joseph Hooke (died 1736), who shared the dismay expressed by Hursthouse, provided the booklet with a pastoral postscript in which he pleaded that the churches should acknowledge the seriousness of their condition and do everything possible both to promote unity and to establish healthy church order within the life of their congregations. These two Lincolnshire ministers were not alone in their despondency concerning the General Baptist people at this time. The General Assembly's meetings in London listened to reports of work in the churches from many counties and, as the years proceeded, the story of decline was frequently echoed by representatives from counties far from Lincolnshire. The East Kent churches were divided over a serious local quarrel. Ageing ministers were not being replaced and several churches were left totally

56

without pastoral oversight.[2]

The 1740 London Assembly urged the churches of Kent and Sussex to meet together in association in order to discover an appropriate brother for the office of Messenger among them. The representatives from all the churches in fellowship with the Assembly at that time lamented 'the decay of religion, the abounding of sin, the present dearth' of spiritual life as well as the 'threatening war'.[3] In 1743 the Assembly received a letter from their churches in the west of England urging them to recommend days of fasting and prayer on 'account of the decay of serious religion'.[4] Ten years later, the churches' representatives expressed concern about 'the great decay of religion', especially the neglect both of family worship and the spiritual instruction of children in General Baptist homes.[5] Some of the most serious evidence for decline was to be found in the London churches. The 1738 Assembly urged the London ministers present to do all within their power to 'invite the other churches in town to join with this Assembly', but the 'other churches' were in a state of grave weakness.[6] It is important to trace the reasons for the continuing loss of spiritual vigour among the General Baptists during the middle decades of the century.

Difficulties

Theological disharmony is still the most prominent factor in the story. Christological and Trinitarian controversy continued to divide. A growing number felt unable to subscribe to doctrinal formulations and the life of the churches became seriously fragmented as orthodox General Baptists became increasingly concerned about deviant ideas. In an attempt to safeguard the fragile corporate identity of their churches within the life of the General Assembly, its 1731 representatives, freshly united, agreed that the theological basis of their co-operation should be on 'the doctrine of universal redemption' and the 'foundation principles' of Hebrews 6.1-2. The Assembly decided that, having regard to previous contention over doctrinal issues, all its churches must agree that neither preachers nor members belonging to the Assembly should 'preach, write or urge in discourse, such controversy about the doctrine of the Holy Trinity, which shall be unto the disturbance of the churches' peace'.[7] But those churches which had not joined the Assembly, including congregations in Buckinghamshire and Northamptonshire, as well as the strategic White's Alley church in London, were reluctant to identify themselves with others who appeared to restrict the free declaration of biblical teaching. The White's Alley church allowed the churches to use its premises for their London Assembly,[8] but did not send representatives to the annual meetings until the article about preaching controversial Trinitarian sermons was removed.[9] When the Assembly did so in 1735, the churches in Buckinghamshire and Northamptonshire also came back into the life of the Assembly.[10]

It is clear from the discussion regarding this article of union that there was widespread aversion on the part of the churches to the idea of subscription to any doctrinal formulation compiled by men. The representatives frequently insisted that the only appropriate language to be used in expounding doctrine was that found within scripture itself. When the Assembly addressed the Northamptonshire churches on the matter, its members explained that it was 'not from a disbelief of the doctrine of the Trinity as contained in the scriptures, that we decline signing of articles but to prevent human explanations being imposed upon us, as if of divine authority'.[11]

The issues were much the same as those which divided dissenters at the Salters' Hall controversy in 1719. Several who refused to subscribe were orthodox in their beliefs but, for some at least, non-subscription was a stage on the route to eventual unbelief concerning the Trinity. This was certainly the case with the General Baptists as the century moved on; an increasing number of ministers came to doubt the traditional foundations of the doctrines of the Trinity and the deity of Christ. The lack of theological unity became seriously disruptive and weakened the structures of denominational life.

A further reason for decline can be traced to recurrent disagreement regarding outworn traditions. Hymn-singing continued to dominate local, regional and national discussions. The theologically orthodox General Baptists of Northamptonshire were unhappy that churches in different parts of the country had 'fallen into the way of singing psalms of David, or other men's composures with tuneable notes and a mixed multitude'. The fact that the voices of believers were mingled with those of unbelievers appears to have been a serious hindrance to some who declared that this 'way of singing' was 'wholly unwarrantable from the Word of God'. General Baptists with these convictions were affronted that those who thought otherwise were not rebuked by the Assembly. The traditionalists were sure that it was the Assembly's responsibility to 'watch against innovations which do easily find a way into the churches of Christ'.[12]

The Assembly replied to the Northamptonshire criticisms by assuring them that only a few churches permitted hymn-singing, but that the representatives would not be happy to deny them the fellowship of the Assembly since such believers were 'sincerely persuaded that they ought to praise God in that manner'.[13]

In the mid 1750s the question of singing was once again before the Assembly. The Turner's Hill church in Sussex raised serious objections both to the practice of singing psalms and reading sermons. In reply, their attention was drawn to the earlier decision about congregational freedom in such matters and they were provided with a copy of the Assembly's tolerant decisions in both 1733 and 1735.[14] The latter Assembly had affirmed that the 'singing of psalms is frequently mentioned in the New Testament', noting that 'the difference is not about singing, but the manner of doing it, whether with musical notes and conjoined voices, or otherwise'. The churches had been urged to adopt realistic attitudes about such points of difference: as 'things appear in different lights to different persons, such a concord' as the traditionalists demanded 'is rather to be desired than expected in this world'. In that the biblical view on such issues 'does not appear clear to us all', there must be room for variation of conviction.[15]

Large numbers of General Baptists continued to be unhappy about the singing of hymns and psalms long after the practice had been widely accepted and profitably used by their Particular Baptist contemporaries.[16]

The Turner's Hill church's further complaint about the reading of sermons[17] may be drawing attention to another threatened departure from earlier practice. The emphasis on spontaneity expressed in extemporary preaching had given way in some places to the use of a prepared manuscript. This may well reflect not simply the accommodation of some General Baptists to the conventions of the time, but also a concern to define doctrinal views with precision in a period of theological unrest. To possess a copy of what was said was a safeguard when any man might be accused hastily, even unjustly, of heterodoxy.

A further example of change in General Baptist traditionalism in the middle decades is found in continuing discussions concerning marriage to Christians outside their own denomination. In 1744 the Bessels Green church sought the advice of the Assembly concerning the problem of 'mixed' marriages. The response of the Assembly is of special interest in that it demonstrates not only a gradual departure from earlier General Baptist endogamy, but also offers an example of the denomination's firmly held connexional ecclesiology. The Kent church's members presented a particular pastoral problem concerning marriage discipline to the London Assembly, but the representatives pointed out that, as the 'case has not yet been laid before any association' locally, it was not proper for them to pass an officially considered corporate judgment. The normal procedures for discussion and appeal were to be carefully and meticulously pursued. The national representatives were on their guard lest any decision of theirs might appear to usurp the rightful procedure of local association debate and advice. Until the problem had been fully discussed within the Kent churches, they 'don't think fit to enter upon it'.[18] These churches considered themselves bound in corporate life with their neighbouring churches and submitted to appropriate structures within their denominational life. Associations were so important and closely-knit among the General Baptists that in 1733 the associated Northamptonshire congregations, meeting at Buckby Mill, could describe themselves as 'the Church of Christ in Northamptonshire'.[19] Association meetings were not simply occasional gatherings of like-minded church representatives; they were an essential corporate expression of General Baptist inter-dependency. It was only appropriate to discuss a local church issue nationally if it had first been brought to the attention of the local region's association meetings.

The Bessels Green pastoral question concerning their mixed marriage case could not be debated on the floor of the assembly, but the representatives thought it appropriate to ask their highly respected Messenger, Matthew Randall, to prepare a detailed reply to the Kent enquiry. His letter indicates a more relaxed attitude to pastoral issues of this kind, though it would not be right to infer from this that his more tolerant outlook was widely accepted within the General Baptist churches of the mid-eighteenth century.

Randall made it clear that 'Mixed marriages are not only inexpedient but dangerous, and sometimes lead to very bad consequences'. From a pastoral point of view, however, once such a marriage has taken place, the church was compelled to take some action. At this point, his itinerancy among different congregations had painfully revealed that 'there may be circumstances full of aggravation'. It is clear from Randall's advice that the fierce outbursts of some General Baptist leaders on this topic were often motivated by genuine compassion for the unmarried women in their churches. Some 'marry out of the church', it seemed, 'through mere worldly interest'. A male member, for example, attracted by the prospect of a more lucrative dowry, might deliberately choose a partner outside his own church 'when there are in it, at the same time, those who, on all other accounts, are equally, if not more deserving'.

The rest of his pastoral letter is evidence of a gradual change of heart on the subject, at least on the part of some General Baptists in positions of pastoral leadership.

Randall maintained that their traditional interpretation of the Pauline injunctions was 'very insufficient'. He was not content merely to repeat the apostle's words as a conventional endogamist shibboleth; contextual issues were important. The frequently quoted apostolic saying 'apparently relates to the Corinthians joining with the pagans at their religious feasts and in their idolatrous rites', and 'Only in the Lord' (I Corinthians 7.39) could surely 'mean no more than in the profession of Christianity, in opposition to the pagan unbelievers'. He pointed the way forward to a more reasonable and compassionate approach to the subject. Was it always wrong for a General Baptist to marry a Christian believer outside their churches? After all, in Corinth itself, 'there were the sects and divisions among the christians yet there is nothing in scripture to forbid their intermarrying'. Similarly, within Judaism there were different groups 'as opposite to each other as those of the Christians' but, although they were forbidden to marry unbelievers, it would 'be hard to find the least intimation in the scriptures' that such diverse Jews 'might not marry into their different sorts'. Likewise, there is nothing in the New Testament to suggest that Christians might not 'marry with those other christians who had, in some material points, departed from the simplicity of the Gospel'. Randall was persuaded that such cases were highly relevant to their discussion and 'seem to mitigate the hard thoughts we have been apt to entertain of those who have transgressed in the affair under consideration'. He was convinced that, if there was 'no direct prohibition' that the early Christians might marry 'pious Jews who believed in the true God but had not as yet embraced the Gospel, then I think your controversy is entirely at an end'.

Randall was concerned about pastoral care as well as biblical precedents. He was clear on the matter of excommunication, in his view a totally inappropriate form of disciplinary action for cases of this kind. It was neither 'a proper method to reclaim offenders', nor would such harsh measures 'promote the Baptist interest'. His peripatetic ministry among the churches of southern England had provided Randall with sad evidence of many people 'who, on account of such severity have never returned to communion, or sought after it', whilst sensitive and compassionate treatment had been used to bring over the 'adverse' partner in such a marriage 'to baptism and communion with the Church'. He knew, moreover, that because of the legalistic approach of General Baptists to the subject, some young people had refrained from joining their churches. Randall was too closely in touch with the realities of life to maintain a rigid outlook. There were good Christian women in their congregations who 'have no offers from among the men of their own community'. He asked what they were expected to do: 'Must they, on pain of excommunication, refuse every sober, virtuous Christian-like person merely because he has not happened to be baptized by immersion or profession of faith? Is this consistent with Christian charity and forbearance?'

In a moving passage, Randall said that, when lovers meet, 'their agreeable mien, complexion, or deportment, often create such mutual liking, and affection, as shall render marriage almost necessary and unavoidable'. The Messenger knew from extensive pastoral experience that without 'this liking and affection ... the true ends of marriage are seldom answered; the persons are rarely happy'. The fact that their partner is a fellow church member is of little consequence. Randall was convinced about the matter; outworn traditions were best abandoned. Members of General Baptist churches should have freedom: 'the case of marriage cannot be brought under any one strict invariable rule by the Christian church'. He firmly believed that much of the earlier discipline might have been sadly misguided, not to say spiritually and emotionally damaging. In his view, 'censures' concerning marriage were 'seldom useful, never commendable, and often hurtful'. The different times called for 'kindly instruction, due caution, friendly admonition, and prayer to God'.[20] The days of inevitable excommunication were gradually drawing to an end. Sadly, however, by that time, in many homes the traditionally rigid marriage ethic had already taken its severe toll. The church's disciplinary action in the form of social ostracism had sometimes led to apparent loss of faith. Randall's persuasive arguments were biblically, pastorally and psychologically well-founded, but there were homes in southern England where the damage was beyond repair. General Baptist marriage traditions did little to encourage young people to identify themselves with these shrinking, insular communities.

The decline in General Baptist life in the mid-century period was also due in part to inadequate ministerial leadership. The Assembly's resolutions were frequently punctuated with anxious references to their need for a salaried or at least partially supported ministry. It is clear from their national discussions that two problems combined to create a serious leadership crisis in their churches: their limited number of ministers were largely without worthy financial support, and the few they had were not being replaced by young men with acceptable gifts. The 1732 Assembly urged every church to 'raise what money they can annually in the best method and send the same by their elder or representatives to the association with a view to supporting the present ministry'.[21] In the following year the Assembly agreed to channel its gifts through the fund earlier established by the London Paul's Alley ministers, Joseph Burroughs and James Foster, and others, for the support of the ministry and for theological education.[22] In 1737 a circular letter was sent out from the Assembly explaining its management, arrangements clearly modelled on the Particular Baptist Fund. Annual collections were to make possible not only the support of 'poor ministers (chiefly in the country) who are elders, or stated preachers', but also to help young ministers purchase necessary books. The wording of this letter appears to anticipate a negative response from some congregations concerning the provision of books. Some of the more traditional churches might well have been resistant to the idea that such external aids were considered an essential part of a minister's resources. If churches were willing to make payments to the fund for ministerial support but not ministerial education, then the Assembly hoped it would not 'hinder them from sending up their collections and gifts; since they may, in all respects, order how their money shall be disposed of'.[23] The circular letter met with an excellent response and the 1738 Assembly, noting with pleasure that the appeal had 'met with good success in some places', urged that its contents be made known more widely throughout the denomination.[24]

Pastoral work was far from easy for these ministers. Many

were compelled to earn their living at a full-time occupation. Those who worked on the land might well have been able to give many spare hours to the service of these communities during the relatively slack periods of the year, but from early spring to late autumn most of them would have had little time to devote either to sermon preparation or pastoral care. Young men were urgently needed for pastoral work. The 1732 Assembly gave serious thought to the matter of improving 'spiritual gifts'; elders and ministers were to do all within their power 'to raise up and encourage all gifted brethren' for the work of the ministry.[25]

By the early 1770s the Assembly faced another problem concerning the ministry; once again it had become seriously worried about the offensive social attitudes and poor moral standards of some of its pastors and church leaders. The London meetings of the General Baptists in 1771 discussed a report submitted by the Messenger, Gilbert Boyce (1712-1800), on behalf of the Lincolnshire churches. It expressed its concern that some of the Assembly's ministers were 'countenancing and encouraging card playing, horseracing and dancing'.[26] The observation illustrates the divergent life-style of some General Baptist people during the second half of the century. The Assembly informed the Lincolnshire Association that such pursuits did not have the approval or encouragement of the denomination's ministers, but there can be little doubt that the other-worldliness of earlier General Baptist congregations was, in some places at least, beginning to change to a pattern of life which their forefathers would have found alarming.

Encouragements

The problems of theological confusion, outworn traditionalism and inadequate leadership are not, however, the whole of the General Baptist story at this time. The denomination made strenuous efforts to provide their churches with a renewed life. The achievements are not outstanding, but they must not be forgotten.

Their awareness of the spiritual contribution of the *family* is an important feature in this period. Acutely conscious of the shortage of young people within their churches, the 1732 Assembly noted with alarm 'a very great decay of holiness and piety in many of the members of the baptized churches'. They were particularly concerned about the 'rising generation' and maintained that the absence of young people was largely due to the failure of Christian parents to conduct family worship. General Baptist leaders at this time were at pains to emphasise the role of the family as an educative unit within the life of the churches. Ministers were exhorted to preach on the subject of the 'pious and religious education of children' and the place of catechetical instruction within family life, to encourage family worship and, by visiting homes, to do all within their power to ensure that parents were frequently reminded of their spiritual responsibility to bring up their children 'in the nurture and fear of the Lord and to acquaint them betimes with the doctrines and principles of the Gospel'.[27]

Twenty years later, the Assembly returned to the same theme. Still concerned about 'the great decay of religion', the representatives particularly asked 'masters of families' to 'concern themselves in the instruction and education of their children and dependants'. The Assembly suggested that the evening of each Lord's Day might provide General Baptist families with a suitable opportunity for worship and teaching within the home. In most rural areas Sunday services would naturally conclude well before dark and the Assembly believed that the closing hours of the day of corporate worship might well be used profitably if members would 'keep their family together to the end they may perform their duties' in this important matter.[28]

The importance of church *discipline* was also stressed within the life of the churches. The 1755 Assembly believed it would be specially helpful if Francis Stanley's *Gospel Honour and the Church's Ornament* could be republished, so the Chatham minister, Samuel Neal, revised the book for a new reading public. Stanley's book, first issued a century earlier, had been reprinted in 1713. Initially available under the title *Christianity indeed* (1655), the book maintained that 'the well disciplined Christian' was 'the delight of Christ'. Its author, a Northamptonshire Messenger, had insisted on the necessity of 'gospel-order' as a vital ingredient in healthy church life, 'governing and being governed, as the children of one Father'.[29] In the mid-eighteenth century, at a time of declining moral and spiritual values, the General Baptists sought to remind one another, through the republication of this important book, of the disciplinary aspects of their ecclesiology.

Decline

By the middle years of the century, some of the churches appear to have become exceptionally weak. In many places numbers had seriously declined. With dwindling congregations, the remnant which remained was always in danger of lowering its standards; disciplinary procedures would be the first to be affected by diminished attendances. The representation of churches at the 1737 Assembly was poor enough for its representatives to draw the attention of the General Baptists to the requirement to send delegates to the London meetings each year. The Assembly also appealed to 'the pastors and ministers of the churches to fulfil their ministry', particularly 'to be diligent in maintaining sound doctrine and good discipline'.[30] In the following year the Leighton Buzzard minister, Thomas Brittain, preached to his people on Psalm 50.15, 'Call upon me in the day of trouble...'; the occasion was 'a solemn fast day on account of the declining state of religion' and the war with France. Brittain was an able minister. A few years earlier he had served the Assembly as its scribe and he was well aware of the low spiritual condition of many churches. In 1749 he went to preach at Caldcot, but records in his diary: 'when I came thither there was none to hear me, so I returned home that night, quite disappointed, sadly tired and sorely vexed'. A few years later, the same thing happened again, this time at Leighton Buzzard: '1755, Feb.23 ... On that day I went to Leighton, and when I came there there was nobody to hear me. So I came home sorely disappointed'.[31]

Brittain's frustrating experiences may have been uncommon, but are not likely to have been unique. The General Baptists at this time were certainly in need of renewal and the decision of their leaders to recall their people to fresh commitment and earlier disciplinary principles was understandable.

Poorly attended churches and declining values caused some members to seek fellowship elsewhere. By the mid-century the appeal of the Evangelical Revival was evident in many parts of the country. In 1742, when Thomas Brittain went to London, his convinced Arminianism did not prevent him from attending the Tabernacle on a May morning to hear 'the famed Mr Whitefield, the Prince of Methodists, a zealous, affectionate, awakening preacher'. On the following day he returned there, this time to hear 'Mr Humphreys[32] ... also a Methodist' and Brittain says that he 'liked him pretty well'.[33] Ministers like Thomas Brittain could not identify with

66

George Whitefield's Calvinism, but they were attracted to his evangelistic zeal and vigorous preaching ministry in the churches.

Some General Baptist members found Methodism far too attractive to limit their attendance to the occasional service; they transferred their allegiance to those communities which had been touched by the revival. By the mid-1740s the influence of both Whitefield and Wesley was beginning to affect the life of the General Baptists. The Lincolnshire churches were peculiarly open to this through Wesley's Epworth associations. Many members were drawn away despite the fact that the county's churches were warned in 1745 that Methodism's 'faith and practice' was 'contrary to the holy scriptures, and to the peace and welfare of their societies'.[34] General Baptists who attended such meetings were sternly reminded that they would be disciplined by Church-Meeting, but for many the temptation was too strong to resist, whatever the consequences. Nor was the defection of members to Methodism confined to Lincolnshire. The Horsham church book tells a similar story of the revival's influence in Sussex. In that church's list of members at this period the entry 'gone to join the Methodies' is found against several names.[35]

It would be a mistake, however, to imagine that Methodism only served to deplete the ranks of the General Baptist churches. The revival's extending influence was also used to quicken the life of many congregations and to this important aspect of the story we must now turn.

The New Connexion of General Baptists

In various parts of the country, Christian people who had been touched by the revival met together in one another's homes for mutual support and to sponsor evangelistic work among their neighbours. The story of some of these groups in Leicestershire is of special importance for, with appropriate encouragement, they were gradually drawn into the life of the General Baptist community. The story begins with the preaching of David Taylor,[36] a servant in the household of Selina, Countess of Huntingdon, the friend of George Whitefield, as well as to a lesser degree of Wesley, and patron of so much evangelical activity in the late eighteenth century. Taylor began to visit neighbouring villages for the purpose of evangelistic preaching and soon gathered a group of small congregations eager to hear and share the message of the revival. One of Taylor's converts was a Leicestershire farm-hand, Samuel Deacon (1714-1812), later to become a leader amongst the General Baptists.[37] The vigorous preaching of these people was bitterly resented by some of their contemporaries. Their meetings were frequently disturbed, their preachers attacked by angry neighbours and legal proceedings taken against them. Despite continuing opposition, those who were influenced by the revival met regularly for worship and in 1745 a meeting-house was built in the village of Barton Fabis. Other congregations began to be established as the Leicestershire preachers travelled beyond the county's boundaries with their evangelical message. By the mid-1750s these churches came to adopt believer's baptism without, it seems, any direct influence from neighbouring Baptists. The work expanded into Derbyshire, Nottinghamshire and Staffordshire, new meeting-houses being built to accommodate the growing congregations. By 1760 these various societies were organised into five churches, led by ministers who were all engaged in secular occupations. Close relations were encouraged between the churches. The ministers met each month for mutual encouragement, and quarterly conferences were held for all members at one of the five churches. In the space of twenty-five years the combined membership had grown from an initial seven to a total of 900 within six churches, and this despite frequent outbursts of fierce local persecution.[38]

Whilst this Leicestershire movement was developing, the revival was exerting its influence in the life of a young man in Yorkshire, later to become the General Baptists' most outstanding evangelical leader. Dan Taylor[39] (1738-1816) began preaching among the Methodist societies around Halifax in 1761, but became unhappy about some of the features of Wesleyan doctrine and pastoral practice as taught by the West Riding Methodists. Although his mentors wanted him to meet Wesley with a view to becoming an itinerant preacher, Dan Taylor left their ranks and soon established a new cause at Wadsworth, near Heptonstall. A small meeting-house was opened where he conducted Sunday services and used the premises during the week for a school which he served as teacher. Taylor was joined by other people who, though indebted to the revival, were not attracted to local Methodist societies. While considering the best form of church order, Taylor and his colleagues came to adopt believer's baptism. Local Particular Baptist ministers were reluctant to baptize an avowed Arminian, but Taylor was told about the General Baptists in Lincolnshire. He travelled on foot with his friend and colleague, John Slater, in order to be baptized, and in

February 1763, at the Nottinghamshire village of Gamston, was immersed in the river by the General Baptist minister, Joseph Jeffries. In May of that year, Taylor attended the Lincolnshire Association meetings and was further exposed to General Baptist life. Later in 1763, Taylor was ordained as a General Baptist minister by the Lincolnshire Messenger, Gilbert Boyce. The following year, in the course of his journeys, Dan Taylor was brought into contact with the five Leicestershire churches which had grown from David Taylor's Barton Fabis initiatives. Although these churches practised believer's baptism, he found them unwilling to identify with the Lincolnshire Association due to the unevangelical views and outdated traditions maintained by some of the Lincolnshire General Baptists. In 1765 and again in 1767 Taylor represented the Lincolnshire Association at the General Baptist Assembly in London. Before long he began to understand the reluctance of the Leicestershire churches; both Association and Assembly were marred by serious divisions over important doctrinal issues. Following joint discussions with like-minded friends in Lincolnshire and the Leicestershire churches, Taylor and his colleagues resolved to form a New Connexion of General Baptist churches and in the summer of 1770 the new movement came into being. It consisted of the five churches from Leicestershire, strengthened by those evangelical churches which belonged to the General Baptist Assembly but wished to organise their corporate life on a firmly evangelical foundation. The new denomination took formal and friendly leave of the General Assembly, carefully expounding the reasons for their secession.[40] The New Connexion was the fruit of the revival. The Leicestershire preacher, David Taylor, had been won to the evangelical faith by Whitefield's friend, Benjamin Ingham. George Whitefield himself had encouraged Taylor to preach in the surrounding villages.[41] As a youth of fifteen, Dan Taylor had travelled on foot twenty or thirty miles to hear either Whitefield or Wesley during their visits to Yorkshire. Now, in the year of Whitefield's death, this vibrant new work was born. It was to promote a warmly orthodox and evangelistic witness within the General Baptist churches.

From 1770 onwards, the New Connexion and the General Assembly maintained a separate existence, though cordial relationships were maintained between individuals in both bodies. Gilbert Boyce (who had ordained Dan Taylor) remained firmly within the General Assembly, still resolutely defending traditions and as late as 1782 was writing against hymn-singing.[42] With the theologically alert hymnody of the revival to enrich their worship, the New Connexion churches became increasingly unhappy about the General Assembly's congregations with their outdated practices, denominational insularity and theological radicalism.

* * * * * * * *

'Open for everyone'

In the opening decades of the new century the Particular
Baptists had scarcely been a model of unified co-operation.
The divisive effects of the hymn-singing controversy had
been given wide publicity through an occasionally vicious
pamphlet campaign, vigorously pursued for about ten years.
This brittle and prolonged exchange of views did nothing to
encourage close relationships amongst the churches.
Moreover, we have seen that on more than one occasion the
Barbican church's theologically mixed membership had proved
a stumbling-block to co-operative ventures. It excluded them
from the 1689 Particular Baptist Assembly, embarrassed the
revived London Association (1704-6) and prevented their
participation in the Particular Baptist Fund. Appalled by the
impression of unloving insularity which the Barbican's
exclusion from the Fund would create outside the
denomination, Stinton pressed for tolerance; did the Baptists
want to be known as Christians 'of an uncharitable and
party spirit'? Did its managers wish to act 'as a sort of
inquisition, for the trial of men's principles in religion'?[1]
But Stinton and the wealthy Barbican Hollis family, who
supported his conciliatory efforts, were lone voices; the
Fund was to be restricted to Calvinistic churches and
ministers and there was to be no compromise on the matter.

During the opening decades of the eighteenth century the
relationships between the two groups of Baptists in the west
of England were not marred by this 'uncharitable and party
spirit'. There, initially at least, the Calvinistic Baptists
appear to have been less defensive, and General and
Particular Baptist leaders met frequently together. Caleb
Evans observed that the Western Baptist Association was 'for
many years kept up by the *Baptists* as such, without any
regard to their different principles in other respects'. He
confessed, however, that eventually 'unhappy differences
arose between the Calvinistic and Arminian ministers',[2] so,
in 1733, they settled upon a Calvinist basis of faith for their
Association life; from that time on the 1689 Particular Baptist
Confession of Faith provided a common theological framework
for their fellowship and discussion. Inevitably, the General
Baptists withdrew.

It is significant, however, that there was greater
tolerance in other parts of the country. The difference is

important. London's most influential Particular Baptist ministers were to adopt a heightened and intensified form of Calvinism as the years went by, whilst congregations in the west and north of the country preserved and shared their Calvinistic faith without recourse to extremes. A moderate form of Calvinism owed something of its continuing vitality to the academy at Bristol. Its influential Presidents and tutors encouraged their students to read widely and did little to promote the theological views extensively publicised through the writings of John Gill and John Brine (1703-65).[3] Their interpretation and application of the biblical doctrine of grace forced a distinction between 'high' and moderate Calvinists in the mid-century period and it is important to trace the roots of this 'high' Calvinist teaching.[4]

Theology

In 1722 a theological work appeared in London's bookshops under the title *Divine Energy*. It was to spark off a controversy which inhibited closer partnership between Particular Baptist churches for most of the century. The book consisted of sermons preached by John Skepp, a Particular Baptist minister who had been converted under the persuasive ministry of Joseph Hussey,[5] an Independent preacher in Cambridge whose views are best described as 'high Calvinism'. Skepp had been a pastor of the church which met in Currier's Hall, Cripplegate, and for about ten years, prior to his death in 1721, had exercised an effective ministry in London. His book revealed that under Hussey's influence he had come to believe that it was improper to use any form of 'moral persuasion' in presenting the claims of the Christian Gospel. In other words, no preacher had the right to invite his hearers to put their trust in Christ.[6] Hussey claimed that only a 'half-hearted Calvinist' would engage in such a work, 'a piece of robbery against the Holy Spirit'. Hussey's teaching was uncompromising and extensively argued in his *God's operations of grace; but no offers of grace* (1707). Skepp made these restrictive views his own.

We have already mentioned the troubles which marked the beginnings of John Gill's ministry in London. When Gill was eventually 'ordained' to the pastorate, one of the participating ministers was John Skepp. When Skepp died, Gill bought most of his books on Hebrew and rabbinics. In 1751, when republishing Skepp's book, Gill says that its author was 'personally and intimately' known to him. The links between the two men were close and the influence marked. Long before Hussey and Skepp, the ideas they shared had been known as an embarrassing aspect of English Calvinism. The sermons of Tobias Crisp (1600-43) had propagated similar views and their republication in 1690 had caused a storm within London dissent.[7] Crisp's teaching so exalted the initiative of God in human salvation that it appeared to sever the nerve of moral responsibility. Christ's saving work, he claimed, ensures that the elect sinner is *already* justified, independent of any significant action on his part. The teaching had some vogue in Particular Baptist churches during the persecution period for, as we have seen, its tenets were raised in questions to the 1689 Assembly representatives, though strenuously resisted. When revived Crispian teaching disturbed and divided dissenting ministers in the late seventeenth century, the London Independents published *A Declaration of the Congregational ministry ... against Antinomian errors* (1699). One of these 'errors' was: 'That ministers of the Gospel ought not to propound the offers of salvation unto all those to whom God calls them to preach, seriously inviting them to improve the means of grace that they might be saved'.[8]

Skepp's teaching, popularly and persistently expounded by John Gill, was Crispianism in a fresh guise. For our purposes it is important to note that, although Stinton's successor in London, Gill proclaimed a form of rigid Calvinistic doctrine which Stinton would not have recognised as the evangelical Calvinism of his own predecessors in that pastorate. Benjamin Keach, for example, regularly and effectively pleaded with his congregation to put their trust in Christ. His winsome evangelistic appeal, found both in his exposition[9] and hymns,[10] did not in any sense compromise his convictions about election and predestination. By contrast, John Gill and his contemporary, John Brine, insisted that it was not appropriate for any preacher to 'offer' Christ. Their preoccupation with election thus became seriously detrimental to persuasive evangelism, and the warm exhortations of earlier preachers were replaced by the intricate expositions of high Calvinism. An admirer of Gill, and one of his successors in the same pastorate, Charles Haddon Spurgeon (1834-92), said that in his 'method of address to sinners', Gill 'cramped himself, and was therefore straitened where there was no scriptural reason for being so'.[11]

By 1737 the propriety of inviting the unconverted to trust Christ was becoming a divisive issue within paedobaptist as well as Particular Baptist churches. In that year, the Rothwell Independent minister, Matthias Maurice, published an important pamphlet which was to bring the subject to the forefront of theological discussion. His *A Modern Question modestly answered* asked whether God makes it

> the duty of poor unconverted sinners, who hear the Gospel preached or published, to believe in Jesus Christ?

Maurice's response to the question was to assert that 'God does by His Word plainly and plentifully make it the duty of unbelievers to believe in Christ'. He insists that no man or woman 'who hears the gospel preached can justly say' Christ did not die for them, and added that it would be 'a great sin in any one to say so'.[12]

A series of continuing publications gave 'the modern question' a secure place on the theological agenda for many years to come. Whenever evangelical ministers came together the subject was constantly under discussion and unhelpful polarisation followed. Subscribers to different viewpoints were speedily labelled and their arguments summarily demolished. Those who insisted on 'offering' Christ's gospel were categorised as 'Arminian'[13] and their high Calvinist opponents were dismissed as 'Antinomians'. Usually the detrimental tags were inaccurate (as when the latter was used of Gill and Brine),[14] though the descriptions fitted some extremists in both cases.

Brine became minister of the Cripplegate church in 1730 and was theologically in the same high Calvinist tradition as Skepp. He entered the debate in 1743 with his *A Refutation of Arminian Principles delivered in a pamphlet entitled, the Modern Question.* Brine dismisses his opponents' views as 'Arminian tenets',[15] but moderate Calvinism did not lack eloquent interpreters within the ranks of the Particular Baptist leadership. The Yorkshire minister, Alvery Jackson (died 1763),[16] was committed to the view that a balanced evangelical theology demanded uninhibited proclamation with clear 'offers' of salvation in Christ, and his book, *The Question Answered* (1752), made his aversion to high Calvinism unmistakably clear. In the following year John Brine responded with an appeal for unity. His *Motives to love and unity among Calvinists who differ in some points* makes oblique reference to Jackson's fervent evangelisation. His own position was poles apart. Brine was persuaded that the elect are united to Christ *before* their personal act of trust in him; both their adoption and their justification precede their experience of faith. As we have seen, it was this concept of justification as prior to faith which the 1689 Particular Baptist Assembly rejected as an unbiblical and unhelpful item of obscure theological speculation.

Brine knew, however, that the Calvinists must close their ranks. The quarrels were a poor testimony. His 1753 tract is evidence of serious concern about division over 'the Modern Question'. He believed that Calvinists of all shades should identify a common enemy in rationalist theology and not dissipate their energies by in-fighting. He urged both parties to recognise 'how numerous they are already, who oppose those important principles, wherein you are agreed, and that the number of such is increasing every day'. He appealed to both the moderate and high Calvinists alike:

> Surely you may allow one another liberty of thought and freedom of modest expression upon those subjects about which your conceptions are not exactly alike. [17]

It is not difficult to identify the increasing number of those who opposed 'those important principles' on which both groups of Calvinists agreed.

Strenuous opposition to evangelical teaching had come from the rationalist theologians and preachers of the period. The doctrine of the Trinity was constantly exposed to virulent attack. John Gill had written against Socinianism in his *Doctrine of the Trinity stated and vindicated* (1731). We have seen that at the beginning of his London ministry Gill was determined to keep the theologically mixed Barbican church out of the Particular Baptist Fund. Subsequent events proved that to some extent his fears may have been justified. The Barbican preachers, John Gale and Joseph Burroughs, were non-subscribers at Salters' Hall. Gale's orthodoxy was never in question but Burroughs, like many others opposed to subscription, gradually moved away from his earlier orthodoxy. James Foster, [18] their successor in that pastorate, embraced a theology which would have been as offensive to many General Baptists at the turn of the century as it later was to Gill and Brine. There was little in Foster's preaching which would encourage any of his hearers to think of God in Trinitarian terms. Gill could argue that, if Foster's teaching was typical of the General Baptists in the middle decades of the century, then there was more than Arminianism which kept them apart. Gill's deep theological concern for his own denomination was also expressed in 1731 in his *Treatise on the Doctrine of the Trinity designed to check the spread of Sabellianism among the Baptists*. The unorthodox tendency of General Baptist ministers like Foster was kept under constant surveillance by Brine and Gill. Brine's *Vind. ation of Natural and Revealed Religion, in answer to Mr James Foster* (1746) is a typical exposure of unorthodox theology, attacked from firmly based biblical and Calvinistic convictions.

John Gill and John Brine were men of immense influence. Without doubt, their ministry, extended by voluminous writings, was used to preserve conventional biblical teaching at a time when the acids of rationalism were damaging the churches. Unfortunately, at the same time they diverted the thinking of many Particular Baptist ministers into patterns of occasionally abstruse high Calvinism and caused the good news to be a matter for arid debate rather than confident proclamation. Spurgeon knew that theology of that kind had 'chilled many churches to their very soul', leading them 'to omit the free invitations of the gospel, and to deny that it is the duty of sinners to believe in Jesus'. [19]

The Independent minister, Abraham Taylor, Gill's fellow participant in the orthodox Lime Street lectures (1730–31), was certainly going too far when he described 'eternal justification' as an 'immoral conceit', [20] but he was not the only dissenter to recognise the danger of any form of teaching which interpreted the Gospel in coldly legalistic terms and minimised the necessity and wonder of an effective personal response to the evangelical message. For a period of about fifty years, high Calvinism robbed many of the Particular Baptists of the warm, evangelistic appeal which had characterised the preaching of men like John Bunyan and Benjamin Keach. In 1748 Whitefield told Doddridge that 'sweet invitations to close with Christ' were 'the very life of preaching', though he observed that anyone who introduced the note of entreaty into a sermon would soon be 'dubbed a Methodist on account of it'. [21] Inevitably, in an atmosphere of this kind the points of meaningful contact between high Calvinism and the Evangelical Revival were few and far between.

Revival

It will be helpful at this stage to explore the relationships which did exist between the Particular Baptist people and the leaders of the Revival. Some Particular Baptist people were openly critical of the 'awakening', while others were inspired both by its vitality and by its message.

The Revival's inspiration came from outside the country as well as within it. The Wesleys had been touched by the German Moravians. George Whitefield had brought news back to England of a remarkable spiritual revival in America through the work of Jonathan Edwards. In 1737, deeply stirred by their own reading of the 'awakening', Isaac Watts and John Guyse brought out an edition of Edwards' *A Faithful Narrative of the Surprising Work of God*. Edwards had described the 'extraordinary dullness in religion' at Northampton, New England, and the change that followed so that by 1735 'the town seemed to be full of the presence of God ... the congregation was alive in God's service'. When Watts and Guyse presented the story to English readers, the preface made no secret of their longing that similar things might take place at home:

> Never did we hear or read, since the first ages of Christianity, any event of this kind ... it gives us further encouragement to pray, and wait, and hope for the like display of His power in the midst of us.[22]

As the book began to circulate, a large number of Christians in the dissenting churches would have agreed with its confession that 'pride and perverse humour of infidelity, degeneracy and apostasy from the Christian faith'[23] had seriously damaged English religious life. The account of a changed situation in New England naturally encouraged evangelical ministers to cherish the hope that things might be different in old England too.

Among the Particular Baptists there were many who longed for a spiritual awakening. The Western Association continued to meet throughout the eighteenth century, but its annual letters constantly draw attention to the disheartening conditions of church life. The 1740 letter urged its readers to acknowledge their spiritual danger and set aside four fast days during the year at which the letter might be read publicly and pondered by the members.[24] The same recommendation about quarterly fast days was repeated the following year, but the leaders grieved that few churches appeared to take any notice of their serious warnings. The churches continued to be in a low condition in the late 1740s[25] and by 1761 Isaac Hann confessed that they were 'almost at a loss to know what we can further say for the stirring up of sleepy professors'. The readers of the

> lest they sleep the sleep of death ... look over the letters which of late years you have had from us ... hearken to the counsel and advice of those who would not cease to warn every one with tears.[26]

Later in 1765, when it was Benjamin Francis's responsibility to write the letter, he commented, with unconcealed grief, on 'the lukewarm and careless' people in the churches who had 'grown formal in the worship, and indolent in the service of God'. Francis asks what has happened to rob them of love and life:

> Is the love of Jesus changed? Is his beauty faded ... or [has] the Redeemer's gospel been deprived of its vivifying energy?[27]

Nor was this lethargy confined to the west of England. Four years later, Daniel Turner (1710-98) of Abingdon wrote to his friend, the London minister, Samuel Stennett (1727-95), expressing his deep concern about the Particular Baptist people whose spiritual life was, in his view, markedly 'upon the decline':

> Useful solid ministers are taken away, and few likely to fill up their places. Many churches are destitute.[28]

There was certainly need for revival but, despite the circulation of Jonathan Edwards' dramatic narrative about 'the conversion of many hundred souls',[29] it was some time before the awakening began to affect the life of the Particular Baptists. Wesley was hastily dismissed by them because of his unqualified Arminianism and Baptists were warned about attending Methodist meetings. The members at Wapping agreed in 1741-42 that participation in 'religious societies or bands', or in a Methodist 'Love Feast', was to be regarded as 'disorderly' conduct, and in 1753 the Norwich congregation declared it 'unlawful for any so to attend upon the meetings of the Methodists'.[30] Even the Calvinistic Whitefield was under suspicion by some; the high Calvinists among them were disturbed that, with persuasive eloquence, he had taken every possible opportunity to 'offer' Christ to his contemporaries.

Wesley's description of predestination as 'the horrible decree'[31] was offensive to all Calvinists, even moderate ones. In the late 1730s there were serious differences on the subject between Wesley and Whitefield. In 1740 Wesley recognised that there were 'bigots both for predestination and against it'.[32] He also told George Whitefield that 'no Baptist or Presbyterian writer whom you have read, knew anything of the liberties of Christ', a comment which Whitefield naturally regarded as a sad reflection of 'narrow spiritedness and want of charity'. He asked whether Wesley had not read anything helpful in Bunyan, Matthew Henry, John Flavel, Thomas Halyburton, or in 'any of the New England and Scots divines'.[33]

The emotive language used by Wesley in his frequently published *Journals* did nothing to endear him to the Baptists. Whenever he had contact with them he made a point of describing them by the pejorative term 'Anabaptist'.[34] Moreover, his impression of Particular Baptists will scarcely have been helped by the attacks made on him by Anne Dutton (1692-1765).[35] She had spent some formative years as a member at the Cripplegate church, noted, as we have seen, for its high Calvinist teaching. On her second marriage to the clothier, Benjamin Dutton, she moved to Huntingdonshire where her husband became minister of the church at Great Gransden. Anne was widowed again in 1747 and gave herself to almost incessant writing. Although she produced numerous evangelical works, she devoted an unusual amount of her time to attacking (as well as befriending) the leaders of the revival,[36] Howel Harris[37] being one of the few to escape a Dutton harangue. Despite his convinced Calvinism, Whitefield was treated to some adverse comments as well as her more obvious Arminian opponents, like John Wesley. One wonders how she managed to remain on such good terms with an Independent minister of wide sympathies like Philip Doddridge.

Although Anne Dutton gave polemical expression to the Gill-Brine school of Calvinistic teaching, this trio did not speak for all the Particular Baptists. There were those who did not share their resistance to the evangelistic message of the revival and who noted with gratitude that the work of its leaders transcended denominational barriers. The revival's impact on Baptist life in Yorkshire, for example, was extensive. The General Baptists' leader, Dan Taylor, first ventured into print with a verse-tribute to the Anglican evangelical, William Grimshaw,[38] to whom the Particular Baptist minister, John Fawcett (1740-1817), was equally indebted. Converted at sixteen under Whitefield's ministry, Fawcett spent the early years of his Christian life within the Methodist societies and for a two-year period regularly walked over to Haworth to hear Grimshaw preach. The young Fawcett became convinced about Baptist doctrine through his contacts with three men who were all Grimshaw's converts: William Crabtree, James Hartley and Richard Smith. Fawcett was later to write the biography of John Parker[39] (successor of Alvery Jackson in the pastorate at Barnoldswick) who owed his conversion to Grimshaw's exposition of the 39 Articles.[40]

Yorkshire was greatly in need of spiritual awakening at that time. When Grimshaw moved to Haworth, many of the parishes in the West Riding were without a resident minister. Half the clergy had responsibility for more than one parish, less than half the churches had two services on a Sunday throughout the year, and 128 of the 903 churches in the diocese of York did not even have one service every Sunday of the year.[41] Many of Grimshaw's converts found their way into newly-established Baptist churches. James Hartley formed a Baptist church in Haworth itself. Although occasionally dispirited by what appeared to be Baptist 'sheep stealing', there were times when Grimshaw could joke about it, playfully complaining, 'so many of my chickens turn ducks'.[42]

Grimshaw's influence, like that of his fellow Anglican, Henry Venn at Huddersfield, was largely confined to Yorkshire, but George Whitefield travelled throughout the country and his impact on Baptist life was evident in many places. His forthright evangelistic ministry made a deep impression on several men who were to become leaders among the Particular Baptists in the mid and late eighteenth century. Andrew Gifford (1700-84) once met a friend who asked him whether he was on his way to hear Whitefield preach in his Tottenham Court Road chapel. He replied positively, explaining that he was going to light his 'farthing rushlight' at the evangelist's 'flaming torch'.[43] Not long after the death of Whitefield, Gifford edited a volume of sermons by the great preacher.

Gifford's debt was not to Whitefield alone. His father, Emmanuel Gifford, minister of the Pithay church in Bristol, had provided him with a fine example of persuasive evangelistic preaching. William Bagley, his co-pastor, recalled that at the close of his sermons, Emmanuel Gifford would 'offer Christ to sinners and invite them to embrace him as offered in the most affectionate and pathetic manner'.[44] Andrew Gifford was also on friendly terms with other leaders in the revival, like William Romaine and A. M.

Toplady who often came to hear him preach, as well as the Welsh leader, Howel Harris.[45] On Gifford's death, the high Calvinist preacher, Richard Burnham (1749-1810) a fellow minister in London's West End, published an elegy in which he recalled

> When'er he preach'd, love stream'd thro' ev'ry text,
>   And all his soul was on the Saviour fix'd ...
> O how he spake of Jesu's matchless charms,
>   And welcom'd sinners to his tender arms.[46]

A naval officer who heard that welcome was Samuel Medley (1738-99).[47] Under the combined ministry of Whitefield and Gifford, Medley was converted while staying in London recovering from a wound. He became a member of Gifford's influential Eagle Street church and opened schools both in London and later at Watford. Medley was to communicate the message of the revival not only by preaching but also through the medium of his many hymns. On moving to a Liverpool pastorate, he became a leader amongst the Baptists of Lancashire, sharing in a ministry to the Northern churches with another hymn-writer, John Fawcett. The developing work of the Yorkshire and Lancashire Association owed an immense amount to their joint inspiration and initiative.

The Cambridge minister, Robert Robinson (1735-90),[48] was another Particular Baptist leader whose life was transformed through the influence of Whitefield. As a young man he regularly attended the famous preacher's London services and, after listening intently to Whitefield's eloquent ministry for about three years, was brought to personal faith. He told Whitefield that he first attended the famous Tabernacle 'pitying the poor deluded Methodists, but came away envying their happiness'. That joy became his own on a Sunday in 1752 and he forever kept the day, 24th May, the same date as Wesley's Aldersgate Street experience fourteen years earlier, as his spiritual birthday.[49]

From the beginning of Whitefield's evangelistic itinerancy, a number of Particular Baptists invited him to their meeting houses. As early as June 1739 the Baptist minister at Hertford asked him to preach in the locality, which he did, three times in the open air, to thousands of people. In the Midlands, a small group of Baptist ministers welcomed him to Bromsgrove where, on one afternoon, he preached outdoors and then went to the Baptist church for an evening meeting. Nor was it only ministers who were eager to support him.

The Seward family at Evesham and the Blackwells of London were also indebted to Whitefield and deeply influenced by the message of the revival. The Seward brothers, Henry, William and Benjamin, were all brought to warm evangelical faith through 'Methodist' preaching. Indentification with Whitefield's ministry sometimes exposed Baptist laymen to serious hazards. One of the Seward brothers was killed at Hay-on-Wye for his participation in field preaching. Another mob attacked Whitefield and his Baptist supporters when they visited Minchinhampton. The great preacher often challenged those who disturbed his meetings and would not allow them to go unchecked; the leaders of the Minchinhampton violence were compelled to pay damages.[50]

Education

Fawcett and Medley were converts of the revival but, although inspired by its heart-warming message, they recognised the importance of solid learning as well as authentic experience. The self-educated John Fawcett[51] laboriously acquired a firm knowledge of Hebrew and Greek. Early in his ministry he met several times a week for theological study with Dan Taylor (the man who was to lead the General Baptist New Connexion) and Henry Foster, an Anglican evangelical who later became curate to another leader in the evangelical revival, Gifford's friend William Romaine. Fawcett the Calvinist, Foster the Anglican and Taylor the Arminian gave themselves to reading schemes which included the classics as well as divinity. The fact that they met so often says much for Fawcett's generous and peace-loving temperament, as well as his passion for serious study. Fawcett's congregations at Wainsgate steadily increased and many spiritual demands were made upon him. Alongside his preaching and pastoral ministry, and like many of his ministerial contemporaries, he helped to support his family by teaching pupils at a day school. John Sutcliff (1752-1814) was one of those who eventually found their way into the ministry. Sutcliff had studied Latin with Dan Taylor and went on to Wainsgate to receive the necessary training from Fawcett to prepare him for a place at Bristol. Young Sutcliff came from a poor family and could only reach the academy to commence his course if he made the 200 mile journey on foot. This he did, in the depth of winter, though it took him a week. After his Bristol training, Sutcliff went on to the pastorate at Olney where, eventually, he too received students for ministerial training. Sutcliff was to be associated with Andrew Fuller (1754-1815), John Ryland (1753-1825), William Carey (1761-1834) and the other

Northamptonshire men who initiated the work of the Missionary Society.

The first of Fawcett's students, and one who shared Sutcliff's passion for missions, was Abraham Greenwood (1750-1825).[52] Like Sutcliff, he too was present at the famous meeting on 2nd October 1792 which initiated the Society's work. Son-in-law and disciple of Alvery Jackson, Greenwood went to study at Fawcett's newly-established academy at Wainsgate, Hebden Bridge, to equip himself for the ministry. Sutcliff's enthusiasm for his studies at Bristol inspired Fawcett and Samuel Medley to initiate the work of the Northern Education Society (1804) which promoted ministerial training in the north of England. After a pastorate in Rochdale and a period in which he established a new cause at Coseley in the Midlands, Greenwood settled at the Oakham church, then part of the Northamptonshire Association. One of the initial thirteen subscribers to the Particular Baptist missionary enterprise, he represents the emerging moderate Calvinist, well-trained and keenly evangelistic - a pioneer spirit with informed missionary zeal.

The Particular Baptists in London were also concerned about theological education in the mid-century period. A meeting of twelve of their ministers in 1752 agreed to the formation of the 'London Baptist Education Society for assisting Students'.[53] Gill, Brine, Edward Wallin and Joseph Stennett II (1692-1758) were among its original supporters. For some time Samuel Stennett served as the tutor appointed to supervise the students' work, but the London scheme did not meet with a great deal of success and by the close of the century the Society gave its support to men who wanted financial help for pursuing their courses elsewhere, like Joseph Kinghorn (1766-1832) who, in 1784, chose to study under Caleb Evans at Bristol, and Michael Parker who went to Fawcett's Academy, by that time at Branday Hall, near Halifax.

The education of some influential young ministers in this period was made possible by the generosity of a distinguished Baptist layman, John Ward,[54] Professor of Rhetoric at Gresham College in the city of London. We have already mentioned his name in connection with the school he opened in Moorfields (1710). Born in 1679, the son of a Baptist minister who had suffered greatly during the persecution period, Ward was educated at a private school and rose to prominence in the academic and cultural life of mid-eighteenth-century London. He was a friend of Andrew

Gifford (whom he probably introduced to the British Museum) and also Joseph Stennett II. The latter was appointed trustee of a special fund provided in Ward's legacy for the education of 'a succession of able and well-qualified ministers', but died before he could assume his responsibilities. Good training was made possible by the generosity of those who recognised its importance. In the previous century Richard Baxter told his contemporaries that, though many of them might not themselves preach, they could 'contribute for the maintenance of some to do it', so 'helping to plant and water the seminaries of the Lord'. 'How many souls may be saved by the ministry of one of these?' Baxter asked. 'And how can money be better husbanded?'[55]

Ward shared that same vision and, under the terms of his legacy, two young men between the ages of 14-18, sons of Protestant dissenters (and preferably Baptists), were given a grammar school education in England, followed by an opportunity to study at a Scottish university. Caleb Evans, later tutor and President at Bristol, was the first student to benefit. Joseph Stennett III commenced his studies at Bristol with the help of the fund and, like Evans, continued his education at Aberdeen. Robert Hall, Jnr also went to Bristol as a Ward scholar when only fifteen years of age and then went on to Aberdeen with Stennett. These men were to give distinguished leadership to the Particular Baptist churches, a ministry made possible by Ward's generosity and concern for education.

None of the academies were as influential as Bristol. There, under the leadership of Bernard Foskett, Hugh Evans and his son Caleb, men were trained for the ministry who were committed to serious study as well as to an evangelistic concern which was the natural expression of their moderate Calvinism. Many of these Bristol students brought an outstanding contribution to the life of the churches in the second half of the eighteenth century. Men like John Ash (1724-79) of Pershore, Benjamin Beddome (1717-95) of Bourton-on-the-Water and Benjamin Francis of Horsley were content to serve their respective churches for between forty and fifty years, pouring their entire working ministry into the pastoral care of rural congregations, faithful biblical preaching, the development of association life, the establishment of new causes and, in each case, the composition or publication of hymns. Their devotional hymnology, passion for associating, and evangelistic initiatives helped to divert many churches from high

Calvinism and introduced them to those influences which were powerfully at work in the Evangelical Revival.

Associations

This moderate form of Calvinism, with its vigorous evangelistic activity began to be disseminated among the Particular Baptists at this time through the renewed life of the Associations. The churches' shared commitment to the same message became more widely known through the helpful practice (initiated by the Western Association) of printing association letters for distribution to the churches. Earlier, letters of this kind had normally been written by hand. Now they were all printed and, no longer limited to the affiliated churches, reached widely-separated parts of the country, bringing further inspiration and challenge. Moreover, both the printed letters and association sermons served to alert the churches to spiritual dangers. The first association sermon to be published was that preached by Joseph Stennett II to the Western Association in 1752. He warned the churches of that 'artful and gradual increase of the opposition, which has, of late years, been made to the deity of Christ and the Holy Spirit'. Stennett reminded those ministers and messengers, who had met that summer in Bratton, Wiltshire, that the association had been formed to ensure the promotion of biblical truth, 'that holiness, which is the genuine fruit of true faith', the 'maintenance of regular discipline in the churches, and the increase of christian charity'. [56]

The impact of the revival is clearly evident in his observation that ministers needed to have a living faith of their own and not to be cold communicators of a set of doctrinal ideas. He knew of some who 'have had no true taste of divine things, nor have *felt* any of this influence upon their own lives'. Such people 'may report the faith and experience of others, but it is not their own report', and Stennett was convinced that this 'has done more injury to real religion than can easily be imagined'. [57] The emphasis on 'feeling' was a significant aspect of the revival's message. Wesley's was not the only heart to be 'strangely warmed'. Impassioned preaching and the circulation of printed sermons helped to encourage within the associations the essential partnership of objective truth and subjective experience.

These associations knew that it was unwise to minimise the importance of evangelical teaching. For this reason the Liverpool meeting of the Yorkshire and Lancashire

Association in 1757[58] not only repudiated extreme forms of high Calvinism, but also dissociated itself from the bizarre theology of a Liverpool Particular Baptist minister, the talented John Johnson (1706-91). His followers maintained his unusual ideas in various parts of the country through to the second half of the nineteenth century.[59] Although John Johnson was nurtured in a General Baptist church, he became attracted to the concept of divine sovereignty in salvation and moved towards a more Calvinistic faith. One of his leading colleagues in the Johnsonian churches, Samuel Fisher (1742-1803) maintained that Johnson was 'neither a Calvinist nor an Arminian'. Certainly, when 'the Modern Question' was under serious debate, he opposed Alvery Jackson[60] and wrote as a high Calvinist, but teachers like Brine refused to recognise him as a supporter of their doctrinal position.[61] Johnson's many books were widely distributed and did not merely circulate among the churches associated with him. They gave extensive publicity to his modalist ideas concerning the godhead, millenarian teaching and his highly insular, exclusive doctrine of the church. Not even allowed to fraternise with other Baptists, Johnsonians were expected to 'maintain an isolated position, with regard to all other religious bodies'.[62]

Johnson's speculative teaching also dwelt on such novelties as whether the Incarnation would have been necessary if man had not sinned, and how 'the purposes of grace' would have been 'executed upon the elect even though sin had never intervened'. The young Andrew Fuller was initially interested in some of Johnson's ideas, holding that there 'was something imposing in his manner, by which a young and inexperienced reader is apt to be carried away'.[63] He was quickly disenchanted, however, though others continued to feel its attraction and Johnsonian teaching created division in several churches. In his Western Association sermon (1752) Stennett had urged the churches to be alert to the 'repeated affronts ... on many of the fundamental articles of our holy religion ';[64] it was a necessary warning in the mid-century years.

But, however important, sound doctrine was of limited worth if not matched by evangelical experience. The Yorkshire and Lancashire Association met in Halifax in 1764 just as the young John Fawcett began his ministry at Wainsgate where the church had been recently troubled by Johnson's teaching. The minutes for that meeting show how greatly the association was appreciated by the churches, providing them with a regular forum for the discussion of theological issues, as well as an opportunity for mutual fellowship, advice, correction and encouragement. The letters from the various churches to their 1764 meeting indicate their frustrations and failures, as well as some evident successes.

A Liverpool church (with Johnson as a neighbour) wrote that it regretted its 'languishing condition', but its members 'esteem it a great mercy to be permitted [to be] a member of the association' since they hoped that by this means they might be assured of the prayers of their sister churches and guided through their difficult experience. They regretted that their public worship was 'attended with great indifference' and their 'private meetings for prayer and conference are much neglected, save only by a few'. They referred with great tenderness and appreciation to the ministry of 'their dear pastor' who had been for a long time a 'nursing father unto them under God', but was now elderly with 'decaying faculties'. He had helped them when 'little but confusion was in the church', but they were now praying for an assistant minister who could help in the work.

Exemplary leadership was of crucial importance. Wainsgate reported with gratitude the arrival of a new pastor a month earlier, the young and gifted John Fawcett. Yet even with an experienced minister there was no room for complacency. The Haworth church, happily served by James Hartley, was grieved about 'many instances of lukewarmness in the best and most important things', though they rejoiced that some lives had been quickened, men and women 'whose last works are more than their first'.

This Association Meeting in the north allocated time, as did others, to the consideration of specific issues which were brought to the association from the churches. In 1764 they discussed the value to the local church of 'private meetings for mutual conference on the things of God'. The response indicates that in the mid-eighteenth century some congregations had made imaginative use of Church Meeting and similar opportunities for fellowship, discussion and prayer. One church asked how such occasions could be used to the best spiritual advantage and the detailed answer given to the enquiry is an example of the association's sensitive pastoral care. The churches were told that at their meetings variety is necessary in the choice of topics for discussion. The constant recital of 'Christian experience', for example, might easily become 'burdensome and dulling to the mind':

It is well known that constant repetition of the same thing, and a treading in the same steps, with scarce any deviation, tends to cloy the appetite and benumb the soul.

Such meetings in the local church are designed for 'Christian edification' and therefore the members ought to give themselves to creative discussion 'upon a variety of useful subjects'. It would not be wise to abandon their opportunity for sharing personal experiences; it is considered a 'great advantage sometimes' for members to be 'acquainted with the trials and mercies of their brethren. To hear of their difficulties which are not a few; and how the Lord supports, upholds, and relieves them by the discoveries of his love to them, and the exertions of his power towards them ... Which noble ends or such like, we may reasonably suppose the Psalmist had in view when he said, Come and hear all ye that fear God and I will tell you what he has done for my soul'. It is likely that, though Baptists had their own long traditions of Church Meeting, some of their thinking concerning mutual conference within the life of the local church was influenced by Methodist society meetings, where the sharing of experience was a common feature.

The association considered, however, that at some meetings it would be helpful to turn from subjective experience to the great objective truths of Christian theology. It 'may be proper ... sometimes to talk of some doctrine or doctrines of the Gospel, or some passage of scripture wherein it or they are contained', an exercise all the more necessary 'especially in this day, when it is furiously attacked on all hands by subtle methods and by designing and cunning men'.

This 1764 association meeting suggested that their local church meetings could profitably discuss controversial ethical topics, knowing that there was a wide 'variety of different cases of conscience amongst the people of God, which for want of proper and seasonable solutions, often lie with great weight upon, and deeply distress their minds'. They could also use such occasions profitably to repeat the main ideas of a recent sermon and discuss its practical implications. At other times it might be helpful to read together from 'some judicious book or useful piece of divinity'. Such books 'often are a means of instruction and comfort' to those people who read them in their houses, so why should they not be used for similar ends when the people of God meet together?

JOSEPH STENNETT

JOHN GILL

ROBERT ROBINSON

CALEB EVANS

DAN TAYLOR

ANDREW FULLER

ROBERT HALL

WILLIAM STEADMAN

The association went on to advise the churches not only about appropriate topics for their Church Meetings, but also gave advice about the manner in which the meetings should be conducted. They are to avoid such subjects 'as may tend to jangling', to share their thoughts with a due sense of reverence and not 'glide into a light and frothy conversation and behaviour at such times'. They are to speak calmly because 'when persons are full of anger, they are incapable of expressing their own ideas, and wrath begets wrath'. The meetings must not be too long or 'several inconveniences will attend it, as dullness etc.'

All of the answers given to questions raised by churches at association meetings provide biblical references for a variety of topics. These include how one defines the precise relationship between faith and hope, what is the appropriate discipline, if any, for a parent who neglects to bring children to church, and even whether it is appropriate to have a cooked meal on the Lord's Day. The response to the Sunday dinner question is a model of balanced bibilical interpretation, showing concern both for the health of members who have long distances to travel (when 'want of some warm and strengthening food may prove very detrimental to their health') and for servants and others who might improperly be kept at home if they had to 'prepare meat ... in a sumptuous manner'![65]

Only a few months after these representatives of northern churches met to discuss such issues, another association came into being which was to make the most outstanding contribution to Particular Baptist life and thought in the second half of the eighteenth century. It became known as the Northamptonshire Association, though from the beginning it included a significant number of congregations from neighbouring counties. In 1764, at the initial meeting of ministers in Kettering, when the association was formed, only two of their churches belonged to Northamptonshire; three came from Leicestershire and one from Buckinghamshire. A circular letter, in 1765, invited other churches to join them and do all within their power to 'encourage this attempt to associate together for the strengthening of one another's hands'.[66] Among that letter's twelve signatories were two Leicestershire ministers who in some sense personify the tension between the moderate and high Calvinists of the time, Robert Hall, Snr (1728-91) of Arnesby, and John Martin (1741-1820) of Shepshed.

At the birth of the Northamptonshire Association there was little to divide the two men. John Martin wrote the association circular letter in 1770, choosing the theme of 'Eternal and Personal Election'. He made it perfectly clear that every soul

> that comes to Christ to be saved from hell and sin by him, is to be encouraged; and it is our duty to show them that election is no bar in their way ...The coming soul need not fear that he is not elected, for none but such will be willing to come and submit to Christ; he need not fear being cast out, for his coming is in consequence of God's drawing love...
>
> If then, they that are coming to Christ, are drawn with the bands of love, let us also endeavour to draw them with the cords of a man. [67]

But some years later, as minister of the Grafton Street Church in Westminster, Martin was to align himself with the high Calvinists and strenuously oppose the teaching of his Northamptonshire colleagues. In 1779 Robert Hall, Snr, preached an association sermon, later expanded and published, which gave expression to an evangelistic form of Calvinism, soon to be expounded more fully by another minister of the same association, Andrew Fuller. Hall's *Helps to Zion's Travellers* (1781) was deeply influential in the life of William Carey. It helped to provide the theological impetus for his missionary enthusiasm.

John Martin, on the other hand, became more deeply entrenched in the high Calvinism he had imbibed in Kettering during his youth. For many ministers, however, the appeal of the teaching associated with the earlier Kettering men, Gill and Brine, was beginning to wane and a new day was dawning for the Particular Baptist people. In the closing decades of the eighteenth century, the new group of Northamptonshire leaders was to direct the denomination into prayerful and more vigorous evangelistic endeavour. It was to inspire new initiatives in the missionary enterprise as well as provide fresh impulse for the planting of new churches at home. Robert Hall, Snr, and his colleagues insisted that the 'Modern Question' had been persuasively answered: 'The way to Jesus is graciously laid open for every one who chooses to come to him ... There is no preventative bar in the sinner's way to the Saviour'. [68]

Change

The gradual change in Particular Baptist theology and life from high to moderate Calvinism during the eighteenth century is due to a number of contributory factors.

We have already seen that it is a mistake to imagine that high Calvinism was ever uniformly and consistently maintained within the life of the churches. That many Particular Baptist congregations had never been without the evangelistic strand in their interpretation of Calvinism is evident from the preaching of ministers like Thomas Collier, Benjamin Keach, William Mitchell (1662-1705)[69] and Alvery Jackson. Such men were never afraid openly to invite their hearers to put their trust in Christ.

Moreover, although high Calvinism had forceful exponents and expansive literature, it came to be challenged outside the Particular Baptist denomination as well as within it. The vigorous debate on the 'Modern Question' meant that Independents, as well as Baptists, brought their best minds to the theological relationship between election and evangelism.[70] Discussion with other Christians on these complex, yet highly relevant, themes served to widen Baptist horizons.

Inevitably, the evangelical revival brought many Particular Baptists into direct contact with a form of Calvinistic theology which insisted on the importance not only of preaching to the unconverted, which every high Calvinist was willing to do, but also of offering Christ's mercy with uninhibited compassion.

Furthermore, the education of a rising generation of ministers became the responsibility of men like Hugh and Caleb Evans, John Fawcett and John Sutcliff who had themselves been influenced by moderate interpretations of Calvinism. However impressed their tutors might be with the solid learning of Gill and Brine, there was little hope that their high Calvinism would be given special prominence in the new academies.

In addition, the developing life of the associations gave regular expression to a less insular and evangelistically inhibiting type of theology. Circular letters and printed sermons continually held out the hope of a revived and more effective church life. The high Calvinists, on the other hand, became increasingly suspicious of associating, particularly questioning its biblical warrant. It was not considered 'particularly sanctioned by scripture example as to be necessary to the existence of churches', but thought to have developed out of 'a principle common to mankind'.[71] Institutions, like the association, where moderate Calvinism was not only discussed but applied, were bound to be under suspicion.

Then again, evangelistic Calvinism was to find its way into Baptist thought and worship through the work of a new generation of hymn-writers. Whatever the latest theological novelty, the warm personal element in Christian experience was kept alive in eighteenth-century dissent by hymns, such as Isaac Watts' 'When *I* survey' and Philip Doddridge's 'O happy day that fixed *my* choice'. These were to be joined by hymns from Baptist writers, like Anne Steele (1717-78), who continued to give expression to similar themes in hymns like 'The Saviour calls':

> Ye sinners, come, 'tis mercy's voice,
>   The gracious call obey;
> Mercy invites to heavenly joys –
>   And can you yet delay?

Her well-known hymn, 'Father of mercies, in thy word', breathes the confidence for which many were searching:

> Here may the blind and hungry come,
>   And light, and food receive;
> Here shall the meanest guest have room,
>   And taste, and see, and live.[72]

They were the themes of revival, presented with persuasive assurance: the blind see, the hungry are fed, the lowly will not be rejected, 'new life the dead receive'.

When verses of this kind began to be sung in Baptist churches, the influence of high Calvinist theology was certain to decline.

In the middle years of the century, books containing Baptist hymns and verse, such as the two we have quoted, began to appear in quick succession. The hymns were as eloquent as the sermons. In 1747 Daniel Turner published his *Divine Songs and other poems,* followed in 1750 by a collection from Benjamin Wallin (1711-82), the Maze Pond, London, minister, *Evangelical Hymns and Songs,* then John Needham's *Hymns Devotional and Moral* (1768), and, more importantly, in the following year the *Collection of Hymns adapted for public worship,* edited by John Ash and his close friend, Caleb Evans. Hymns by Watts, Wesley, Doddridge and Anne Steele were included in the 1769 Ash-Evans collection, but the new book also brought the hymns of the editors' fellow Bristol men, Benjamin Beddome and Benjamin Francis, to a wider audience. John Fawcett's *Hymns adapted to the circumstances of public worship* was published in 1782 and within a few years yet another book appeared edited by John Rippon (1750-1836), *Selection of Hymns from the best authors* (1787). Amongst Baptist worshippers, Rippon's hymnal was more popular than all others, passing through more than thirty editions. A newly-liberated Calvinism had found expression in song.

Any account of the change from high to moderate Calvinism needs also to note that, following the death of Brine (1765) and Gill (1771), no other theologian of comparable stature and intellectual ability could take up their distinctive emphases with the same skill and forceful logic. As preachers, they had been eagerly sought after and both men had devoted a large amount of their time to writing. As early as 1737 one London Baptist, offended by Gill's sermon, commented to him in an open letter on 'that itch of scribbling which you are so famous for'. His correspondent, aware that Gill had also written or spoken fiercely against 'the learned and ingenious Mr Abraham Taylor' as well as Matthias Maurice, made the undeserved comment that Gill's heart must be a 'very muddy fountain or it would send forth clearer streams'.[73] Later Robert Hall, Jnr, was to be even more devastating in his complaint. As far as he was concerned, Gill's voluminous writings were a 'continent of mud', books he wished had been written in Welsh so that he would have been spared the boredom of reading them.[74] This biting criticism was hardly just. Gill's work as a commentator on the whole of the Bible was prized and used by hundreds of preachers in the eighteenth century, while his three-volume *Body of Divinity* provided ministers, students and others with an exposition of Calvinistic theology which gave them confidence at a time when, in a rationalistic age, biblical doctrine was under attack. Under the influence of preachers and writers like James Foster, ministers and churches could easily pass from doctrinal freedom to theological indifference, and then to Unitarianism. Gill and Brine helped to keep many a reader in the way of truth when others were hopelessly confused. Given the limited perspective, theirs was a contribution to eighteenth-century theology which did not deserve Hall's censures and ought not to be so summarily dismissed and forgotten. But Gill and Brine lacked natural successors. When, on Gill's death, the Southwark pastorate became vacant, three names were under consideration, each of them from the 'moderate' Calvinist wing - John Fawcett, Benjamin Francis and John Rippon. Fawcett responded to the church's invitation but, after his farewell services, did not have the heart to leave his people at Wainsgate. He withdrew his acceptance and remained in Yorkshire, possibly marking the occasion by writing the hymn, 'Blest be the tie that binds'.[75]

Benjamin Francis received an unanimous invitation in 1772, was keenly attracted to the 'pleasing prospect of more extensive and general usefulness', but he too could not bring himself to forsake his congregation even though they were not able fully to support him. The deacons of the Carter Lane church informed Francis that 'Dr Gill about a year and a half before his death proposed to lay down the pastoral charge' if they could get the Horsley pastor to succeed him, adding that Francis 'was the only one he ever could have thought of'.[76] That Gill himself was more than happy for Benjamin Francis to follow him suggests that some high Calvinists had come to recognise that amongst the majority of able ministers the 'Modern Question' had not been answered in their favour.

In the event a young Bristol student, John Rippon, filled the vacancy and served as the church's pastor until 1836. Its members were aware that their new minister's Calvinism had different overtones from Gill's and, on Rippon's arrival, some high Calvinists, with their fellow members' 'cordial approbation and consent',[77] left to form a new church in Dean Street. They invited an even younger man to be their minister, William Button (1754-1821), whose father had been one of Gill's deacons. Button was later to emerge as a vociferous opponent of Fullerism[78] but, by the opening decades of the new century, preachers and writers who disliked Andrew Fuller's theology were a steadily decreasing minority.

In contrast, moderate Calvinism had many lucid interpreters. Andrew Fuller belonged to a company of men who were unashamed debtors to the high Calvinist tradition. They had welcomed some of its best themes but had also identified its most glaring omission. The good news of God's electing sovereignty and undeserved grace was not a message to be treasured selfishly within the narrow confines

of exclusivist churches. Abraham Booth's *Reign of Grace,*
Robert Hall's *Helps* and Andrew Fuller's *Gospel Worthy of all
Acceptation* each made it unmistakably clear:

> None can in truth say they desire salvation, but may
> not apply for it or cannot attain it.
> The gracious grant is indefinite, the way to Jesus is
> open and free for whosoever will without exception. [79]

* * * * * * * * *

EXPANSION   1770 – 1815

The parting of the ways

The removal of the New Connexion's congregations left the old General Assembly largely bereft of evangelical witness. Several churches, as well as outstanding leaders, hoped that the two groups might come together again and a new basis be found for a revived, integrated corporate life. Gilbert Boyce constantly worked for such a union and, on the New Connexion side, Dan Taylor clearly hoped at one time that the two groups might find a common basis for unity. But the quest for union was perpetually frustrated. Some of the 'Assembly' churches, expecially those in Lincolnshire, resolutely insisted on the old traditions. Touched by the revival, the New Connexion churches were certainly not going to abandon hymn-singing. The fervent evangelicalism of the mid and late eighteenth century had been expressed in song, to the great enrichment of the New Connexion's worship. Moreover, the imposition of hands upon newly baptized believers had little significance in the churches recently united under Taylor's vigorous leadership. It was not simply that the Assembly was suspicious of the New Connexion's indifference concerning traditions; the Connexion itself had serious misgivings about the Assembly's theological laxity. Attempts to bring the two bodies closer together were often frustrated when some form of proposed doctrinal agreement found its way on to the agenda. The Assembly insisted that the only necessary theological basis for union was the 'six principles' of Hebrews 6.1-2 and their Arminian commitment to 'general' rather than 'particular' redemption. [1]

Troubled about doctrinal laxity, Taylor's churches had drawn up six articles[2] which embodied some of their common convictions and paid special attention to some aspects of truth, like the deity of Christ, which had earlier caused theological disruption within General Baptist life.

It is important to observe that, although Taylor was prepared to compose the agreed articles, not all his New Connexion colleagues were happy about doctrinal subscription. Looking fearfully in the direction of some sound but inert high Calvinists, the New Connexion believed it more important to insist that its ministers had a personal experience of Christ than a precisely defined creed.[3] But increasing doctrinal indifference within the life of the

General Assembly forced the two groups further apart. The exact relationship between the two groups in the late eighteenth century is not easy to determine, but it is clear that from 1786 onwards the General Assembly firmly believed that the New Connexion's churches were in some form of union with the Assembly.[4] Certainly from this time on Dan Taylor and others represented their churches within Assembly life until 1803, when doctrinal difficulties compelled them to withdraw.[5] The General Assembly's minutes for 1786 rejoice that 'the Leicestershire Association', as Taylor's churches were known, had declared 'their willingness to unite' with the Assembly and that they would send their representatives to the Assembly each year.[6] The New Connexion's printed minutes of that same year make no reference whatever to the union, yet Gilbert Boyce strongly maintained that the New Connexion's churches were in fellowship with the Assembly. Inevitably embarrassed by the Assembly's early nineteenth-century acceptance of unitarian ministers, the New Connexion's first historian, Adam Taylor (1768-1833), makes no mention of the alliance. For our purposes it is best to consider the two groups in isolation. Whilst some New Connexion leaders, like Dan Taylor, frequently took a leading part at General Assembly,[7] the links between the two groups became more and more tenuous as doctrinal indifference became a determined characteristic of the General Assembly's relationships with its ministers and churches.

The General Assembly churches

When the New Connexion came into being, the General Assembly's churches seem to have been in a numerically encouraging position. Messengers were urged to visit the churches to assess their spiritual condition and they reported increased numbers in 1775, 1777 and again in 1788.[8] But gratitude for larger congregations in certain places did not mask the concern expressed by some leaders for the spiritual life of their congregations. In 1772 the Cranbrook church asked the Assembly 'to enquire into the causes of the decay of Christian piety' and make suggestions about remedying the situation.[9] Twenty-six years later the Canterbury church expressed its anxiety about 'the declining state of religion' and the Assembly agreed to set aside a summer Sunday as 'a day of fasting and public prayer' in order to 'humble themselves before Almighty God'.[10]

Several members of the Assembly were convinced that the serious shortage of ministers lay at the heart of their problems. Year after year, as the messengers, elders and representatives gathered in London for their annual meeting, specific churches were mentioned which were totally without pastoral oversight. Moreover, as the years went by, the elderly messengers became difficult to replace. The need for additional messengers[11] and ministers[12] frequently appeared on the Assembly's agenda. It was not difficult in these circumstances to persuade the Assembly that the training of ministers should become its most urgent priority. In 1786 the churches were urged to encourage appropriately gifted young men seriously to consider 'the work of the ministry'.[13] In 1792 the Assembly appointed Stephen Freeman of Ponders End as tutor for ministerial training and the churches were asked to give financial support to this important educational initiative.[14] However hesitant the Assembly may have been doctrinally, its concern about an educated ministry was commendable; in this respect its enterprise preceded the formation of the Particular Baptists' venture in the Northern Education Society (1804) and also the New Connexion's London Academy (1798). Freeman trained one student only through 'the General Baptist Society for the Education of Young Men for the Ministry', but the need continued and in 1794 a committee was formed to manage affairs.[15] John Evans[16] of the Worship Street church, Islington, where the Assembly held its London meetings, became secretary of the Society. In the following year he accepted responsibility as tutor.[17] Evans had been educated at Bristol under his relative, Caleb Evans, and Robert Hall, Jnr, before going to Aberdeen and Edinburgh Universities for further study. Academically well-equipped for the task and keenly interested in education, Evans opened a local school where he taught for thirty years despite the serious physical handicaps of later life. His work as tutor of the Academy (1795-1818) meant that a considerable number of General Baptist ministers were taught by him. Evans wrote over forty books, but his theological views were hardly orthodox. *A Brief Sketch of the Several Denominations* (1795) was his most popular work, but he was criticised for thrusting 'his Socinian sentiments into almost every article'.[18] His tutorial leadership at the academy played some part in encouraging the thinking of the Assembly and its ministers in the direction of the more rationalist and unconventional patterns of theology.

Another feature of the Assembly's life was its continuing concern for General Baptist work overseas. In the late eighteenth and early nineteenth centuries several members of their congregations chose to emigrate and begin life afresh in a new land; in 1796 the Bessels Green church reported that 'many' had left for America.[19] The awareness of new opportunities abroad must have been quickened in some instances by the Assembly's interest in the churches of Virginia and South Carolina.[20] The Particular Baptist minister and editor, John Rippon, had provided information about American Baptists in the first volume of his popular *Baptist Annual Register*. In 1790 there were 'a number of General Baptists' in Kentucky[21] whilst 'nearly one half [of] the inhabitants of both Virginia and North Carolina are Baptists'.[22] The *General Baptist Magazine* began to publish news of American work and the Assembly appointed representatives to maintain links with General Baptist people in that country. Both Dan Taylor and John Evans were among the regular correspondents. It was natural for the General Baptists to encourage such links and, wherever possible, respond to the appeals which came for their financial support.[23] After all, with the exception of those in Pennsylvania, most of the first Baptist emigrants were General, rather than Particular, Baptists. Many of those early American churches whose local history is known to us numbered some immigrants from England amongst their founding members.[24] As the nineteenth century dawned, an increasing number of English Baptists were to make their way across the Atlantic.

The Assembly's social concern is another commendable feature of its late eighteenth century life. Troubled about gambling and its consequent financial deprivation, the Assembly stated its view that 'gaming is evil'. Whilst they acknowledged that it was inappropriate for the churches 'to examine minutely into the private practice of all' their members, the Assembly's representatives testified strongly against 'unlawful games',[25] recognising that many people who habitually indulged in gambling were not in any financial position to do so; card-playing for money could quickly rob many a home of essential food and clothing. In the eighteenth century, England was 'gripped by gambling fever'. Parson Woodforde regularly played for money.[26] The wealthy lost thousands of pounds at card-playing and huge sums of money changed hands in London clubs. Charles James Fox had lost £140,000 by the time he was twenty-five years of age.[27] The nation's rich citizens might choose to waste their money in this way, but the working class could not afford to take such risks. It was right for the Assembly to express its disapproval.

Understandably, greater concern was expressed over

another social evil, the slave trade. The Assembly eagerly lent its support to the abolition programme. In 1787 it asserted the conviction that trading in human life was totally 'inconsistent with every rational and humane principle' and appointed a select group of representatives, including Dan Taylor, to assure the Committee for abolition of the wholehearted support of the General Baptist people.[28] They had every reason to be concerned. In many places the nation's conscience was deeply stirred. British slave-traders had transported about a million and a half Africans during the eighteenth century. The sugar trade of the West Indies had relied on slavery and by 1790 about £70 million of British money had been invested in the business. Wesley took a firm stand against it and his followers were not alone in refusing to have sugar in their tea because of this iniquitous traffic in human life.[29] Nor were the slaves only to be found overseas. Ill-used people of all ages were brought to England also. The *London Advertiser* for 1756 offered 'a Negro boy age about fourteen years old' for £25. The lad had been 'used two years to all kinds of household work, and to wait at table'.[30] Liverpool specialised in the importation of both tobacco and slaves; the painter, Henry Fuseli, said that he could 'everywhere smell the blood of slaves' in Liverpool, by 1800 the second largest town in England. At one time in the eighteenth century over a hundred ships left Bristol each year on the slave trade with a total capacity of about 30,000 slaves.[31]

Baptists were found in significant numbers in both Liverpool and Bristol. They would be particularly aware of the appalling conditions under which innocent people were transported from one country to another. During transit the sick slave could hope for little help and would probably be thrown overboard rather than nursed to better health. Christian people could no longer be indifferent to such cruelty.

Doctrinal issues frequently emerged in debate as well as social injustice. As the General Baptist people became more committed to rationalist thought, a number of leaders became concerned that the denomination might lose its distinctive testimony. The Assembly found occasion specially to commend notable theological works on the biblical doctrine of believers' baptism and drew the attention of the churches to some important books. In 1788 Joshua Toulmin published an edition of William Foot's study of baptism and the Assembly of that year told its representatives that the book was worthy of 'serious reading and distribution among the churches'.[32] By the early nineteenth century, and following the decisive departure of the New Connexion's churches, the Assembly recognised that their concern to be in harmony with 'free-thinking' theologians might gradually obscure their baptismal teaching and practice. In 1809 they affirmed that 'in addition to the efforts of our denomination in union with other friends of rational religion we recommend frequent conversation and plain preaching on the subject of baptism and also the reading of such tracts ... concerning that gospel ordinance, particularly the small pieces of W. Richards, D. Taylor, S. Kingsford, J. Dobell, W. Kingsford, &c'.[33]

Yet, despite these commendable efforts to educate the General Baptist people in appropriate spiritual, social and theological concern, many of the churches slowly lost their evangelical faith and practical evangelistic outreach. Quickened by the revival, it was inevitable that the New Connexion churches would ultimately sever their tenuous links with the General Assembly and come to develop an independent life of their own. It is important to note how these clearly distinguishable groups within General Baptist life ultimately came to the parting of the ways. The Assembly's movement in the direction of Unitarianism was gradual and a number of events contributed to the change.

The formation of the New Connexion in 1770 was an irritant to General Baptists who did not share its theological convictions. In that year the Assembly expressed its regret that any of their number 'should make any particular sentiments and interpretations of scripture' a reason for separation from their ranks. But, rather than initiate disciplinary or critical measures, they chose to leave the evangelicals 'entirely at liberty to judge and act for themselves'.[34]

In 1777 the Lincolnshire Messenger, Gilbert Boyce, asked for the Assembly's opinion 'as to the reunion of those members who separated from us in the year 1770'. The Assembly replied that the basis for their fellowship must remain as before, their Arminian doctrine of universal redemption and the 'truths as recorded in Heb.6.1-2'. They insisted that, just as they had left their New Connexion friends free to pursue their own doctrinal interests, so they too must be left free not to embrace those ideas. They refused to give up their 'liberty by signing any other articles, to establish such union than those on which the Asssembly has for many years stood'.[35]

We have seen that at its inception, the New Connexion had drawn up six articles which gave clear expression to their evangelical theology. They insisted on the doctrinal importance of the person and work of Christ, the fall of man, the importance of the moral law, salvation by faith, the Holy Spirit's work in regeneration and the duty of believers' baptism.[36] Teaching of this kind became an increasing embarrassment to the General Assembly's churches.

Disillusioned by doctrinal indifferentism, some ministers of the General Assembly had turned to the New Connexion for assistance, support and encouragement. John Stanger[37] of Bessels Green in Kent left the Assembly's church in the village and formed another which, for a while, became part of the New Connexion before Stanger ultimately found the fellowship he was seeking within the recently quickened life of the Particular Baptist churches under the influence of Fullerism. The New Connexion's southern churches had never really enjoyed any appreciable association life; deprived by this isolation, the Eythorne church also went over to the Particular Baptists in 1785.[38]

Constantly denied the supportive ministry of visits from messengers, General Baptist churches in counties such as Leicestershire and Northamptonshire gradually dwindled in numbers and effectiveness, whilst others turned to the New Connexion for pastoral help and encouragement.

At the Assembly of 1784 the New Connexion representatives presented the delegates with 'a proposal of union'. Its suggestions took the form of a letter which made it clear that the Connexion fully appreciated the fact that 'a perfect conformity to one another in every religious sentiment' was not an essential ingredient in associating. The New Connexion was sure that some variants in worship need not fragment the corporate life within the denomination. Could not those previously controversial issues, such as hymn-singing, the biblical authority for the Messenger's office and the imposition of hands upon newly baptized believers be left to the choice and conscience of individual congregations?

The New Connexion's letter went on, however, to explain why many of their members could not find it in their hearts to identify fully with the co-operative ventures of the Assembly:

We speak now of those who deny the proper atonement

of Christ for the sins of men, and that justification before God, and acceptance with him are enjoyed by faith in Christ, and not by works, which we apprehend to be very fundamental doctrines.

They went on to say that theological disunity of this kind made it impossible for them to participate in the denomination's corporate activity, expressed, for example, in the practice of pulpit exchanges, persuaded as they were that the preaching of heterodox ideas 'must have a pernicious influence on the minds of the people'.[39]

Two problems made close union impossible. At that particular time several of the older churches in membership with the General Assembly insisted on retaining some of their outdated practices. The Lincolnshire churches assembled at Boston made their response to the New Connexion's letter by dogmatically asserting the essential continuance not only of the imposition of hands at baptism, but also of the necessity to abstain from eating blood.[40] Gilbert Boyce had worked hard for union within the county and beyond it, but some of his own restrictions were a hindrance to fuller co-operation. His tract, written in opposition to the practice of hymn-singing, had reached the Leicestershire churches which, influenced by the revival, had no intention of sacrificing an inspiring element in their regular congregational worship.

In 1785 the Assembly returned to the New Connexion's letter; their discussion illustrates the second difficulty in the way of closer union. The churches were moving apart not solely because of differences in church practice but, more seriously, on account of divergent theology. The Assembly insisted that union must be on a 'broad basis',[41] which gave its members as much freedom to reject the Connexion's evangelical doctrine as the Assembly had left them free to embrace it.

As we have already seen, the Assembly's minutes record the New Connexion's acceptance of this 'broad basis' in 1786 and certainly from that time Dan Taylor took a leading part in the Assembly's concerns, occasionally presiding at its meetings, sharing its committee work, writing its circular letters and even preaching at its important annual meeting. By this time Taylor had moved from Yorkshire to London in order to become the minister of the General Baptist congregation in Church Lane. Finding himself in closer proximity to other General Baptists in the metropolis and home counties, he naturally encouraged better relationships. He had been absent from the General Assembly between 1767 and 1784, but his new work at Church Lane made attendance more practicable and denominational union more desirable.

It is clear, however, that within a few years the prospect of integration became increasingly remote. The New Connnexion's publications describe the Assembly with increasing detachment. The circular letter of 1793, signed by Taylor, urged the churches of the Connexion to hold frequent conferences for the discussion of spiritual topics and went on to say that it was

> a glaring fact, that among the old General Baptists, *their* cause in many places was nearly extinct, through the inattention of *their* ministers, and others to these measures.[42]

The words hardly convey the impression that its writer belongs to the Assembly, still less that he treasures any confidence in its spiritual future.

Other events were to minimise the possibility of reconciliation. The elderly messenger, Gilbert Boyce, had been a zealous worker for union; his death in 1800 made an alliance less likely. Despite his outdated ideas, he had consistently maintained that the churches needed each other; his younger colleagues in the Assembly did not share either his Trinitarian doctrine or his concern for closer fellowship with evangelicals.

Furthermore, doctrinal tensions were creating serious differences between the Assembly and the New Connexion. Novel theological ideas began to be popularised by Elhanan Winchester,[43] an American preacher who ministered to a London congregation in the late eighteenth century. Winchester gave special prominence to the doctrine of universal restoration and his views rapidly gained acceptance among the General Baptists of the Assembly and elsewhere.

Concerned about the spread of these ideas, John Stanger of Bessels Green wrote two important pamphlets. *The Doctrine of Universal Restoration considered as unscriptural* appeared in 1790, to be followed in 1791 by his *A Short View of the Doctrine of the Trinity as stated in the Scriptures.* Stanger's writings indicate that deviant theology was not peculiar to the General Baptist churches. Tensions had also arisen in Kent and Sussex among the Particular Baptists and Stanger, like others, was deeply concerned.[44] He knew the life of the General Baptist Assembly from the inside. As a minister who had been present at the formation of the New Connexion, he was aware of the serious misgivings of his evangelical General Baptist friends. In 1791 the Kent and Sussex Association of Particular Baptist churches had received Stanger's Bessels Green church into membership; that same year, William Vidler (1758-1816),[45] the young minister of the Battle church, had been chosen as its moderator. Vidler's name was suggested as association preacher for 1793, but by that time his ideas of universal restoration made him unacceptable for such a responsibility. The Battle church was excluded from the Association and fifteen of its orthodox members withdrew from church membership 'declaring their disbelief of the universal restoration of devils and men from hell'.[46] Vidler's name became widely known as a heterodox teacher. On one of his propaganda tours he visited East Anglia where, at Wisbech, he came under the influence of the Unitarian preacher, Richard Wright (a former Johnsonian),[47] and from that time he threw himself whole-heartedly into the proclamation of Unitarian teaching. Vidler's name was to become notorious in the matter of Assembly and New Connexion relationships.

In 1801 two significant events took place at the General Assembly's London meeting. For the first time the New Connexion was publicly criticised. The representatives were offended by the continuing use in some circles of the Connexion's original name, the 'Free Grace General Baptists'. They maintained that the title implied that other churches in the Assembly did not preach the doctrine of God's free grace and that its use was 'injurious to the peace and harmony of the general body & therefore ought to be laid aside'.[48] The comment was certain to aggravate the existing tension. Later in the proceedings a more serious matter was raised; it was agreed that William Vidler be admitted as a personal member of the General Assembly.[49] The combined action of criticising the New Connexion and welcoming an avowed Unitarian was to prove disastrous to already fragile internal relationships.

In 1803 Dan Taylor withdrew from the Assembly[50] and within a few years Vidler was to rise to the same position in its leadership as Taylor enjoyed in the New Connexion. At the same time as Taylor's withdrawal, the Battle church, now General rather than Particular Baptist, applied to join the Assembly.

At the same 1803 Assembly, the representatives asked that either William Vidler or Robert Aspland[51] be invited to serve as Assembly preacher for the following year. With the mention of Aspland's name alongside Vidler's, the transition to Unitarianism was virtually complete. At one time Aspland had belonged to the Soham Particular Baptist church where, earlier, Andrew Fuller had commenced his ministry. After baptism at the London Devonshire Square church, Aspland went to study at Bristol, then on to Aberdeen. Finding himself out of harmony with the teaching of the Particular Baptists, he sought the help of John Evans at the Worship Street church in London, where the General Baptists held their annual Assembly. With Evans' help, Aspland became General Baptist minister at Newport, Isle of Wight, and later declared himself a convinced Unitarian. He accepted an invitation to become minister of the Presbyterian church at Old Gravel Pit, Hackney, where he remained for forty years as an advocate of liberal theology. He co-operated with Vidler, particularly in the editorial partnership of the *Universal Theological Magazine* which, in 1805, was warmly commended to the Assembly's churches. In that year the Assembly invited its representatives to consider 'the importance of free enquiry in matters of religion' and asked that the magazine, unrivalled for its 'impartiality', be 'patronised by all our churches'.[52] In the following year, when the name of the journal was changed to the *Monthly Repository of Theology and Literature,* the Assembly's churches were again reminded of its value and every congregation urged to procure it for wide distribution, particularly among members who might not be able to afford their own copy.[53] Also in 1806 the Unitarian, Richard Wright, and his Wisbech church were welcomed into the Assembly's membership.[54]

By 1813 the New Connexion, disturbed about the spread of Socinian 'poison', urged its churches not to allow any believers in 'that destructive system' to preach in their pulpits.[55] Unconcerned about anxieties of that kind, an 1815 General Assembly Committee reported on the 'success of Unitarianism which, with the exception of baptism, may surely be called the cause of the General Baptists'.[56] It was hardly surprising that, only a few years earlier, some General Assembly leaders had urged their churches to study the doctrine of baptism with care; their distinctive denominational witness was rapidly disappearing in favour of a rationalistic theology which had little room for the repentance, personal conversion, union with Christ and identification with his committed people, expressed in their earlier baptismal teaching and practice. John Burgess, a General Baptist from the Ditchling, Sussex, church, who emigrated to America, accurately reflects the outlook of these churches at this time. Writing to a friend in 1815, Burgess says:

> I think the doctrine of the Trinity one of the greatest corruptions in the Christian Church. The doctrine of the pre-existence of Jesus Christ I have entirely given up ... The doctrine of original sin, of atonement ... are to me doctrines absurd in the extreme. [57]

We must now look at those churches which preferred to adhere to biblical doctrine rather than the novelties of Vidler, Wright and Aspland, and which were equally suspicious of teachers like John Evans and the like, with their less explicit heterodoxy.

The New Connexion of General Baptists

It is important to understand how the churches under Dan Taylor's leadership came to develop their totally different evangelical life.

In the story of the New Connexion it is difficult to exaggerate the increasing momentum given by Taylor's charismatic leadership. [58] He provided the new movement with dynamic continuity. Born in 1738, the year of Wesley's Aldersgate Street conversion, Taylor belonged essentially to the ethos of the revival. As a child of five he worked in the coal-mine alongside his father. Throughout his entire life he continued to give himself to strenuous activity within the life of the churches. Self-educated but widely read, Taylor was a young man of 32 when the New Connexion came into being and was able to bring vision and tireless industry to the service of its people. His views were eagerly sought by the growing churches. In times of doctrinal confusion, their members urged him to visit them so as to guide them into biblical truth and settle their disagreements. In 1782 he was called to the Kegworth, Leicestershire, church when it was affected by Socinian teaching and travelled specially from Yorkshire in order to settle the dispute. [59] Frequently making long journeys in the interests of the churches, Taylor became respected and loved throughout the entire Connexion. No comparable figure within the life of the General Assembly was so widely acknowledged as an outstanding leader.

Taylor's publications were even more influential than his pastoral contacts. As the churches grew in number, it became impossible to form personal links with them all, but his skills as a writer were placed at the disposal of the Connexion. In 1790 his *Essay on the Truth and Inspiration of the Holy Scriptures* appeared; initially preached as an Association sermon, it warned of those theological currents which would cause the Assembly's churches to drift away from biblical moorings.[60] His Circular Letters also drew the attention of the churches to important doctrinal themes and their practical implications. In addition to these writing responsibilities,[61] he edited the *General Baptist Magazine* (1798-1800)[62] which was replaced by the *General Baptist Repository* with its valuable dissemination of church news. The *Repository,* edited by Adam Taylor, first appeared every six months but from 1810 began to be published quarterly.[63]

Concerned about theological education and unhappy about the tuition offered by John Evans to ministerial candidates, Taylor became first tutor of the academy at Mile End which began to receive students in 1798.[64] Some older members of the New Connexion's churches were not particularly happy about courses of study. Earlier, there had been some in Leicestershire who 'looked with suspicion on any other book than the Bible and hymn-book',[65] but Taylor and his colleagues helped the denomination to recognise the importance of sound learning.

Short in stature, but physically strong and robust, Taylor poured his considerable gifts and energy into the life of the Connexion. When one remembers that between the ages of five and twenty-four most of his daytime hours were spent in a coal-mine, his intellectual achievements are staggering. Author of more than forty works, besides Circular Letters, he attended about two hundred conferences, preached at the opening of many new meeting-houses and shared in ordination services and association meetings in various parts of the country. He preached almost every day of his ministerial life and led the denomination in vigorous evangelistic enterprise.

Another factor to be borne in mind when assessing the success of the Connexion is sociological. Many of the new churches were established in or near towns which grew beyond all expectation in the course of the Industrial Revolution. Before the emergence of factories, framework-knitting was undertaken in the cottages of local

110

people, especially in northern and midland communities. These centres often provided ideal sites for the newly-emerging factories and in such localities an increased population was inevitable. In a period of serious financial deprivation, towns which provided secure employment were obviously attractive. With the introduction of the stocking-frame, hosiery became the main trade of Hinckley, which may be taken as an example of local and church development. The New Connexion church in that town grew steadily during the late eighteenth and early nineteenth centuries.[66] Formed in 1766, its first minister, William Smith (an original member of the famous Barton, Leicestershire, church), served until 1798 and during his pastorate saw its membership doubled. He was succeeded in 1799 by Joseph Freeston and by 1809 the Hinckley membership had risen to three hundred. Five years later (1814) the church decided to divide to form new congregations at Thurleston, Earl Shilton and Wolvey.[67] Hinckley's population in the early nineteenth century was in the region of 5,000; of these only 90 were employed in agricultural work as opposed to 2,600 in trade. Stocking-frames were housed in the homes of local people. Housing conditions were appalling and sanitation almost non-existent. Yet from homes of this kind many poor and uneducated people found their way into the New Connexion's growing churches throughout the midland counties, and congregations in Nottinghamshire, Leicestershire, Northamptonshire, Warwickshire and Derbyshire made significant strides forward in both spiritual and numerical growth.

The success of the New Connexion also owes a good deal to the spiritual resourcefulness of its pioneers. Inspired by the revival and particularly by the example of the Methodists, they emphasised the necessity of regular conferences for ministers and church leaders. Although committed to the autonomy of the local church,[68] they knew the dangers of congregational isolation. They proved the value of mutual encouragement, of sharing fresh ideas, as well as of giving practical support and healthy doctrinal instruction to one another, particularly at a time when deviant theologies were seriously dividing many congregations. During this period, the General Assembly's meetings became formal and brief, while the leadership of the New Connexion sponsored a vigorous and relevant association life.

Association life within the Connexion was channelled into evangelistic initiatives and the membership urged to consider how declining causes might be effectively revived. The church at Staleybridge, Lancashire, fell upon hard times in the early nineteenth century, but its services were regularly conducted by ministers from the Yorkshire Association which, in 1815, supplied the small congregation with a new minister. The church was soon admitted to the New Connexion with sixty members and within a year or two they had increased their membership to eighty and commenced a new work at nearby Ashton-under-Lyne.[69] Similarly, the church at Leicester (formed as early as 1651) was by the late eighteenth century in serious decline. An elder of the Earl Shilton church owned the meeting-house there and preached only five or six times a year to a handful of people. Eventually the small company asked the New Connexion to supply them with visiting preachers and the churches of Loughborough and Barton came to their aid. John Deacon accepted the pastoral oversight of the church in 1782 and within twelve months twenty-four new members were baptised and the newly-revived church began to establish preaching stations in the adjoining villages.[70]

Another important factor which aided the growth of the Connexion was the changed theological climate within the life of the Particular Baptist churches. With the increasing acceptance of Andrew Fuller's moderate Calvinism, evangelical General Baptists discovered a new confidence within the wider life of Baptist people. High Calvinism, with its inhibitions about evangelistic preaching, had distanced them from their fellow Baptists. Now they began to feel a common bond of denominational identity. When Fuller's *Gospel Worthy of all Acceptation* was published in 1785, the ministers of the New Connexion urged Dan Taylor to offer informed comment on its leading ideas. In the following year, Taylor's response appeared under the pseudonym 'Philanthropos'. In 1806 Andrew Fuller preached at Taylor's Whitechapel meeting-house, saying that he had accepted the invitation 'to convince the world that perfect cordiality' existed between the New Connexion's leader and himself.[71] By the opening years of the new century special services were being shared by both General and Particular Baptist preachers. When the General Baptist church at Beeston, Nottinghamshire, was opened in 1806, a General Baptist minister preached at the morning service, an Independent in the afternoon and a Particular Baptist at night[72] and, when the General Baptists of Hinckley opened their new meeting-house in the following year, both Dan Taylor and the **Particular** Baptist, Robert Hall, Jnr, preached at one of the services. [73]

Churches of the General and Particular Baptist persuasion were drawn closer together in the early nineteenth century through their common commitment to overseas missions. [74] The *Periodical Accounts* of the work of William Carey, Joshua Marshman (1768-1837), William Ward (1769-1823) and their partners in India, which first appeared in 1794, found their way into the hands of General as well as Particular Baptists. Under Adam Taylor's editorship the *General Baptist Repository* began to publish not only a detailed historical account of the work in India, but also some letters signed 'P. Derby' which urged the General Baptists to form their own Missionary Society. The nom-de-plume hardly concealed the identity of the New Connexion's vigorous advocate of overseas missions, J. G. Pike (1784-1854), minister of the Brook Street church in Derby. A disastrous fire at Serampore in March 1812, leaving in ashes the translation and printing work of almost thirteen years, touched the hearts of General as well as Particular Baptists. The first news of the fire in a letter from Carey's colleague, Marshman, to John Ryland reached England in early September and within three weeks the Derby church had presented the needs of the Serampore missionaries to the General Baptist friends meeting in conference at Loughborough. The churches were asked 'to make collections to assist in repairing the melancholy loss at Serampore' and J. G. Pike was requested to prepare the appeal letter to the New Connexion's churches. Pike also asked Fuller whether their churches could send a minister to work alongside the Serampore team and, if not, whether they might provide financial support for 'a native brother' chosen by Carey and his colleagues 'and to whom they might sometimes write'.

Pike continued to press for greater missionary commitment on the part of his fellow General Baptists. His persistent efforts bore fruit (though not without opposition) at the New Connexion's Association meetings at Boston in the summer of 1816, for at that meeting the General Baptist Missionary Society came into being with Pike as its first Secretary. When William Ward returned to England, the newly-formed Society sought his advice about the best field for their pioneer work and five years after the Society's formation the new work began in Orissa. The impetus was largely the result of the Particular Baptists' missionary initiative. A modified theology, which issued in more vigorous evangelistic enterprise at home and abroad, had served to bring together the General Baptists of the New Connexion and their Particular Baptist colleagues. As the new century progressed, it was to issue in even closer co-operation.

* * * * * * * *

'A glorious door'

For the transformation of their churches in the last quarter of the eighteenth century, the Particular Baptist people were indebted not only to Fuller's theology but to honoured institutions and outstanding leaders. A highly influential theological college, some gifted personalities and their important writings, and a new sense of denominational identity (expressed, not least, in revived associations) all played their part in quickening the spiritual life of congregations throughout the country.

Leaders

Long before Andrew Fuller wrote his books, with their exposition of the more 'moderate' Calvinism which was to take his name, Bristol Academy was teaching its students a similar warmly evangelistic theology. As far back as 1773 (when Fuller was but a young member of the church at Soham) Bristol's President, Caleb Evans, urged one of his newly-ordained students to persuade his Oxfordshire congregation of 'the *ability* of Christ to save; ... to save unto the *uttermost,* to save all that come to God by him. Preach the *willingness* of Christ to save'.[1] In that same year the newly-formed Bristol Education Society had sponsored a 'Gospel Mission' into Cornwall with Benjamin Francis as its itinerant;[2] it was the precursor of more extensive evangelistic preaching in the west of England twenty years later.[3] Caleb Evans claimed that the Bristol Education Society's work was not only to provide a basic theological training for ministers, but also to encourage 'missionaries to preach the gospel wherever providence opens a door for it'.[4] Although the initial impetus for the Baptists' missionary venture was to be provided by charismatic leaders like Carey and Fuller (who had not been trained at academies), men such as John Sutcliff, Samuel Pearce (1766-99), William Staughton and John Rippon, who were to sponsor and support the work of the Baptist Mission, had all been at Bristol.

With the passing of John Brine and the more influential John Gill, the old forms of high Calvinism began to lose their hold. The times were ripe for new leadership. One such leader was Robert Hall, Snr, minister of the church at Arnesby, Leicestershire. In 1779 he preached a sermon at the Northamptonshire Association's meetings from Isaiah 57.14 with its prophetic appeal that certain 'stumbling-blocks' be removed from the life of God's people. For Hall the hindrances were plain for all to see. Many people in the churches were 'stumbled' by doctrinal difficulties; they had been misled by unorthodox ideas about Christ's deity, by disturbing doubts concerning God's changeless love, by spiritual problems relating to the the doctrines of election, union with Christ and the atonement. For others, the problems related to 'practical religion', particularly the nature of the moral law. But the greatest impact of Hall's sermon, published in 1781 as *Helps to Zion's Travellers,* was his section on some 'stumbling-blocks' in Christian experience. Hall knew that the high Calvinist preoccupation with election, reprobation and predestination had created deep uncertainties in the minds of sensitive people as to their ability to respond to the gospel of Christ:

> If any should ask, Have I a right to apply to Jesus the Saviour, simply as a poor, undone perishing sinner, in whom there appears no good thing? I answer yes; the gospel proclamation is, Whosoever will, let him come. [5]

In the course of his exposition Hall had used another Isaianic saying, 'Look unto me and be ye saved all ye ends of the earth' (Isaiah 45.22). On many occasions a young man sat in Hall's congregation at the Arnesby church concerned about other lands. William Carey walked about twenty miles to benefit from his preaching and was to become one of the Association's most famous sons. He claimed that the Arnesby minister's *Helps* was deeply influential in his thinking: 'I do not remember ever to have read any book with such raptures'. [6]

Hall's book secured a unique place in the gradually evolving history of the late eighteenth-century missionary movement. It inspired Carey not only to pursue its leading themes but also to relate them to the needs of people overseas who had never heard the Christian message. In the same year as *Helps* was published, another Northamptonshire Association minister began to write his first book. Andrew Fuller's *The Gospel Worthy of all Acceptation* (1785) provided Baptists with a more detailed exposition of Hall's ideas. Fuller commenced his ministry at the Soham church where he was a member. Robert Hall, Snr, had shared in his ordination. The links between the two men were close and strong. Andrew Fuller was to emerge not only as moderate

Calvinism's eloquent theologian but also as the new Missionary Society's secretary and its most zealous advocate.

In the unfolding story, it was another Northamptonshire minister who brought a further significant contribution to the development of evangelical and missionary concern within the life of the Baptist denomination and beyond. In 1784 the pastor at Olney, John Sutcliff,[7] issued his famous 'Prayer Call'. At the Association's meetings that year Sutcliff made the proposition that churches be encouraged to hold a special meeting on the first Monday evening of every month for united prayer 'that sinners may be converted, the saints edified, the interest of religion revived, and the name of God glorified'. Sutcliff's appeal in the Association's Circular Letter urged its readers not to remain parochial in their praying:

> ... let the whole interest of the Redeemer be affectionately remembered, and the spread of the gospel to the distant parts of the habitable globe be the object of your most fervent requests.[8]

From his youth Sutcliff had come under the influence of an evangelistically uninhibited Calvinism. First a pupil of John Fawcett in Yorkshire, Sutcliff then became a Bristol student and in 1789 reprinted Jonathan Edwards' *An Humble Attempt to Promote Explicit Agreement and Visible Union of God's People in Extraordinary Prayer for the Revival of Religion & the Advancement of Christ's Kingdom on Earth*. In his book Edwards had described a remarkable prayer-movement in New England. Once more (as with the publication of his *Faithful Narrative* fifty years earlier), the transatlantic dimensions of the Evangelical Revival become unmistakably evident.[9] This invitation to special prayer for the increased effectiveness of Christ's work at home and abroad was readily received as several associations began to make it known.[10] It also became, as Sutcliff and his friends had hoped, interdenominational in its impact. Within two years Independent (as well as Baptist) churches in nearby Warwickshire began to organise monthly meetings of this kind[11] which led, in turn, to the formation of the London Missionary Society (1795). Moreover, the 'Prayer Call' was heard in other lands. By the time George Burder, the London Missionary Society's secretary, issued an abridgement of Jonathan Edwards' book in 1814 he knew of similar monthly prayer meetings in Holland, Switzerland, Germany, America, India and Africa.[12] A new sense of urgent missionary concern was gradually spreading through the churches. The effects of Sutcliff's call were to widen the geographical and spiritual horizons of Christians of all denominations in this land and beyond.[13]

Another important leader, also Bristol-trained, was John Rippon.[14] While Hall and Fuller laid the theological foundation for the movement and Sutcliff provided the incentive to prayer, Rippon published inspiring accounts of new life at home and abroad. As the editor and compiler of *The Baptist Annual Register,* he was an enthusiastic collector of Baptist news. Published in 1793, the opening page of the *Register's* first volume carried a print of Caleb Evans, a clear expression of a spiritual debt. The expansionist outlook and missionary objective was clear from the start; below the editor's name on the title page were his own verses:

> From East to West, from North to South,
>   Now be his name ador'd!
> EUROPE, with all thy millions, shout
>   Hosannahs to thy Lord!
>
> ASIA and AFRICA, resound
>   From shore to shore his fame;
> And thou, AMERICA, in songs,
>   Redeeming love proclaim!

Rippon's volumes made the Particular Baptist people deeply aware of one another's work. They contained lists of churches and their ministers by counties. Association Letters often appeared in full, thus extending the theological and spiritual impact of the interdependent life of Baptist churches.[15] The *Register* told the story of associations where there had been a positive response to Sutcliff's call for monthly prayer meetings. It reported on the campaign for the abolition of the slave trade, gave news of Baptist associations in the United States, and printed their circular letters. It provided lists of publications by Baptist and other writers both at home and overseas. Extensive obituaries supplied biographical detail concerning Baptist personalities as well as outstanding leaders from other denominations, in America as well as in England and Wales. Overseas work was given a prominent place. News was there of ministry and mission. in the West Indies, Poland, Germany, Switzerland, the Netherlands, France and Russia. Readers were reminded of the impact of European political events on Christian work and witness. The 'astonishing Revolution in France, and the increasing thirst among the nations after civil and religious liberty', were described and Baptist readers invited to pray that the French people and others 'may also enjoy spiritual evangelical liberty'.[16] Rippon encouraged his Particular Baptist contemporaries to look beyond their association and denominational boundaries; the *Register* informed his readers of the General Baptist New Connexion and supplied minutes of their meetings as well as a list of their ministers and churches. When Caleb Evans died, Rippon not only published an elegy by Benjamin Francis, but also included in the *Register* an informative reading-list which Evans had supplied to one of his students in 1773.[17] In the list Gill is acknowledged as a writer who 'excels in rabbinical learning' and as one who is 'the touchstone of orthodoxy, *with many*'; the qualifying words distance Evans from high Calvinism. He knew that John Owen's works were 'highly valuable for sound learning and genuine devotion', but it is Doddridge who 'is to be valued for sublimity, perspicuity, penetration and unbounded love'. Evans also believed Jonathan Edwards to be 'the most rational, scriptural divine, and the liveliest christian, the world was ever blessed with'. The bibliography has further telling illustrations of the theological influences most forcefully at work in the Bristol tradition at this time.

Mission

In Rippon's information about recent books, one title appeared amongst publications in 1792 which was to do more than anything else to thrust the Baptist people into imaginative missionary endeavour – William Carey's *An Enquiry into the Obligations of Christians, to use means for the Conversion of the Heathen*. It was the work of one of the most gifted, persuasive and influential figures in Baptist history.[18] He was born in the Northamptonshire hamlet of Paulerspury, where his father was village schoolmaster as well as parish clerk. Brought up in the school-house, Carey soon discovered a love for books. Defoe's *Robinson Crusoe* came into his hands while he was still at school. James Cook was making his important voyages and the story of those travels was to fire Carey's enthusiasm for work overseas.

Supreme among all other qualities which Carey possessed was the gift of endurance. The boy's father, 'who discovered no partiality for the abilities of his own [five] children', had to admit that William's special aptitude was 'steady attentiveness and industry'. Mary, his sister, confessed that 'whatever he began, he finished. Difficulties never discouraged him'. Writing to his son, Eustace, years later, Carey shared the secret: 'I can plod', he said. 'That is my only genius. I can persevere in any definite pursuit. To this I owe everything'. It was a characteristic which was certainly needed and often tested. When, as a young man, he preached at the Olney church, the members felt unable to commend him for the ministry on their first hearing. But Carey was patient. He was heard again after a year of waiting and this time they warmly approved him. When he shared his deep concern for the unevangelised with his fellow ministers in the Northamptonshire Association, he discovered that leaders had to be won at home before others could be reached abroad. Fuller tells how Carey's plan to take the Christian message to other nations was first regarded as a wild, impracticable scheme and few would offer him any encouragement: 'Yet he would not give it up, but talked with us *one by one,* till he had made some impression'. He went on thinking, reading, talking and praying for about seven years until a group of formerly apprehensive men felt ready, indeed honoured, to identify themselves with him in the great adventure.

John Rippon's *Register* told the Baptist people that profits from the sale of the *Enquiry* would be devoted 'to the use of a society for propagating the gospel among the heathen'.[19] In the year of its publication, Carey preached the sermon at the Northamptonshire Association's May meetings in Nottingham: 'Enlarge the place of thy tent, and let them stretch forth the curtains of thine habitations: spare not, lengthen thy cords, and strengthen thy stakes ... and thy seed shall inherit the Gentiles, and make the desolate cities to be inhabited' (Isaiah 54.2-3). The divisions of the sermon provided the inspiration for action: Expect great things from God – Attempt great things for God. Something must be done. A plan was to be prepared for the formation of a missionary society to be presented at the next meeting of the Association's ministers in Kettering. In October 1792 these leaders resolved that 'in the present divided state of Christendom, it seems that each denomination, by exerting itself separately, is most likely to accomplish the great ends of a mission, it is agreed, that this society be called, The Particular Baptist Society for propagating the Gospel amongst the Heathen'.

Within a few weeks the initial subscription list of £13.2s.6d had been considerably increased. Another Bristol man, Samuel Pearce, told his Birmingham friends of the venture, formed the first Auxiliary and sent £70 to the next meeting.[20] The work had begun, but not without an apathetic reception among ministers and churches. Samuel Stennett predicted that the mission would come to nothing and counselled London ministers 'to stand aloof, and not commit themselves', advice, said Fuller, which 'was very generally adopted'. Abraham Booth was a keen helper, but his leading deacons were openly hostile. The elderly Benjamin Beddome, sad that Carey had not succeeded him in the Bourton-on-the-Water pastorate, feared that 'the great and good man' would 'meet with a disappointment'. Some churches would not promise their support. It was up to individuals to give if they wished to do so, and Fuller often wept when they did not.[21] Yet, despite discouragements, Carey sailed for India and within a few years other denominations were implementing the same vision. When Carey's first letter from India reached John Ryland in July 1794, he had moved from Northampton to Bristol to become principal of the Academy. Among a group of friends invited by Ryland to hear the letter was David Bogue, who was so moved by what he heard that he shared his missionary concern with readers of the *Evangelical Magazine*. His article, along with Thomas Haweis' detailed review of Melvill Horne's *Letters on Missions,* led to the formation in 1795 of the London Missionary Society. The published *Periodical Accounts* of Carey's work came into the hands of Charles Simeon, the Cambridge evangelical vicar, as well as several members of the so-called Clapham Sect, and this in turn led to the beginnings of the Church Missionary Society in 1799.

The new life which became evident in Northamptonshire did not restrict its interests to overseas missions. At the Association's meetings in May 1792, when Carey preached his famous Nottingham sermon, the local church representatives discussed two other equally important issues on the denominational agenda, the need to abolish the slave trade and the promotion of evangelistic work in England.

The Northamptonshire Association's ministers and messengers insisted, as did their colleagues in the Western Association, on identifying themselves fully with Wilberforce's abolition campaign to remove 'the inhuman and ungodly trade in the persons of men' and allocated the sum of five guineas as an initial contribution.[22] Those ministers who had been trained at Bristol were well aware of the slavery issue. Bristol's merchants had gathered considerable wealth through the 'ungodly trade' and ships sent from the city in the eighteenth century were loaded with cloth and muskets for Africa where they were favourably exchanged for slaves. These traders, 'incarnate Devils' and 'the common enemies of mankind', as Baxter earlier described them,[23] forced helpless African people into crowded ships to work in a strange land. Once in America the slaves were bartered for tea and sugar which was then conveyed back to Bristol. English sailors were known to hate the trade and its associated brutality. Many of this country's merchants did well out of it and Bristolians were among them. Caleb Evans had been outspoken on the subject and had given wholehearted support to the anti-slavery campaign, his well-informed criticism proving an irritant to Bristol's prosperous tradesmen. London, Bristol and Liverpool[24] were the main centres of the trade and in each place Baptists gave expression to a sense of public concern about this inhuman traffic.

In London, the Bristol-trained pastor of the Maze Pond church, James Dore, preached on the subject and then published his sermon, *On the African Slave Trade* (1788). This attracted great attention and by 1790 was in its third edition. Two other Bristol men trained under Ryland, Jacob Grigg[25] and James Rodway, went to Sierra Leone, then familiarly known as 'the White Man's Grave'. Grigg's uncompromising opposition to slavery led to his expulsion from the colony within a year.

When the Northamptonshire Association's ministers and messengers began to launch the work of overseas missions and to participate in the anti-slavery campaign, they also recognised the need for evangelistic work at home. At the 1792 Nottingham meeting money was given to 'encourage the preaching of the gospel at Derby' and a further sum to 'encourage preaching the word at Braybrook'.[26] When Jacob Grigg was on board ship waiting to sail from Sierra Leone to America, he wrote a letter to John Sutcliff of Olney, thanking him for his pastoral concern: 'You were the only person who thought on me'. Sutcliff's thoughts often turned to Christian work in other places. At the same time as he acknowledged Grigg's letter, he wrote also in response to one from John Ryland at Bristol which told of a need in Cornwall where 'the fields are white' and of the plan to send Steadman and Saffery there for a two-month tour.[27]

Influenced by this moderate Calvinism of the Bristol tradition, one of its former students, Benjamin Francis, undertook monthly preaching excursions from his church at Horsley. During a forty-year pastorate he travelled through 'the most uninstructed parts of Gloucestershire, Worcestershire and Wiltshire' and was 'the first means of introducing evangelical religion into many dark towns and villages in all the neighbourhood round'.[28] His journeys extended into Cornwall and across to Ireland where later, in both places, village itinerancy became a significant aspect of evangelistic witness. Robert Robinson similarly had gone out from his church at Cambridge in the 1760s to work in about fifteen neighbouring villages, often preaching at five in the morning and half-past six in the evening to several hundreds who gathered to hear his addresses, subsequently published as *Sixteen Discourses* (1783).[29]

Once Fullerism began to be accepted, its implications for evangelism were eagerly grasped and applied. The Northamptonshire Association's Circular Letter of 1779 endeavoured to promote village preaching and, even earlier, the Western Association had commenced a fund (1775) which, amongst other purposes, would provide support for village preachers. When, during the summers of 1796 and 1797, William Steadman (1764-1837) and John Saffery were preaching throughout Cornwall, their expenses were met by the newly-formed Missionary Society. News of these journeys made by Saffery and of similar ventures by James Hinton (died 1823) of Oxford appeared in the Missionary Society's published *Periodical Accounts*. They provided inspiration for the formation in 1797 of the London Baptist Society for the Encouragement and Support of Itinerant and Village Preaching.[30] This society owed a great deal to the initiative of Abraham Booth,[31] minister of the Prescot Street church in Goodman's Fields, who, after Rippon, was London's most influential minister in the late eighteenth century. The itinerants sent out under the auspices of this newly-established evangelistic agency went into Shropshire, Herefordshire and Wales, and within a short period of time grants were being made to ministers in a large number of different counties who wanted to launch out with evangelistic ministry in areas not yet reached.

In ventures of this kind much depended on the initiative of ministers in the larger churches. In 1797 the Shrewsbury pastor, John Palmer, gave himself to regular preaching throughout Shropshire and within about eight years could write that the church had 'upwards of 70 members that do not reside within ten miles of us mostly the fruits of village preaching'. After only a year in the pastorate at Lockwood, near Huddersfield, its minister, James Aston, could likewise report that village preaching had resulted in forty-four recent additions to the church's membership. John Stanger was equally active in Kent, travelling mostly on foot and establishing a new work in many villages. Robert Imeary, the North Shields minister, reported that in 1809 thirty new members had been added following his itinerant evangelistic work in the surrounding area.[32] Other leading ministers, such as Benjamin Francis and John Saffery, went further afield and visited Ireland in the course of their preaching tours. Francis preached in Dublin on about thirty different occasions.[33] In 1813 Saffery went to Ireland on behalf of the Missionary Society and what he had to share on his return concerning that country's social and spiritual needs led to the formation in the following year of the Baptist Irish Society.[34]

Some of these ministers first recognised the importance of itinerant evangelistic preaching during their college training. Towards the end of his life Bristol's Principal, Caleb Evans, 'most earnestly recommended village preaching' to one of his students. In the late 1780s, when Samuel Pearce was a student at the Academy, he engaged in evangelistic work in the Forest of Dean, spending his evenings 'going from house to house among the colliers ... conversing and praying with them, and preaching to them'.[35] In 1800 another Bristol-trained pastor, John Sutcliff, opened a small academy in his own home at Olney. Young men who went there to train for the ministry at home and abroad were committed to regular itinerancy in the surrounding Northamptonshire and Buckinghamshire villages.[36] In 1805 the newly-formed Baptist academy in Yorkshire invited William Steadman, one of the last of Caleb Evans' students, to be its President. As we have seen, Steadman had been on evangelistic tours throughout Cornwall and naturally encouraged student itinerancy throughout the northern counties.

Education

In 1775 the Cambridge minister, Robert Robinson, told his Church Meeting that 'the baptist cause suffered much for the want of a pious, but far more for want of a learned ministry'.[37] However, Robinson's views were not held by all Baptists. The Welsh minister and historian, Joshua Thomas (1719-97), shared with John Ryland his suspicion that 'perhaps ever since they formed churches here' the Baptists had been 'strongly prejudiced against a learned ministry', adding 'And a considerable degree of that continues to this day' (1795).[38] Robinson was certainly aware of this kind of opposition but, persuaded of the importance of good training, he made an attempt to open a theological academy at Cambridge.[39] Though his ambition was not realised, it is an indication of a deep concern in some quarters for effective ministerial education.

The denomination's oldest academy at Bristol exercised a remarkable influence on the developing new life of the Particular Baptist people in the second half of the eighteenth century. During Bernard Foskett's thirty-year principalship sixty-four students came for training, some of whom were to give outstanding leadership in long pastorates. Foskett was succeeded by one of his former students and later tutor at the Academy, Hugh Evans, who was joined in turn in his leadership at Bristol by his gifted son, Caleb. In 1770 Hugh and Caleb Evans realised that the times called for a more vigorous approach to ministerial training. In the first ten years of this father and son partnership in the Academy they had received about two new students every year. Both men longed to prepare 'able, evangelical, lively, zealous ministers of the Gospel'; they knew that it had 'long been a matter of complaint' that there was 'a great scarcity of ministers to supply the congregation of the Baptist denomination'.[40] The two men told the Particular Baptist churches that some of the students they had welcomed to the Academy had been compelled to abandon their studies because of inadequate financial support. It was to ensure a more reliable provision for such men that the Bristol Education Society came into being in 1770.[41] The Academy was no longer the sole responsibility of the Broadmead congregation, and looked for its support from a wider constituency. The Society made it abundantly clear that 'no man can be an acceptable minister of the Gospel if he be not a converted man, and furnished with those ministerial gifts or talents which God alone can communicate'. Yet they rightly affirmed that, although 'all the learning in the world is, of itself, by no means sufficient to complete the ministerial character', the 'importance of a liberal education ... is so exceedingly obvious, that one might almost think it impossible that any considerate, intelligent person should not be convinced of it'.[42] The Academy's principal and tutor led the work forward with infectious enthusiasm; the curriculum was kept wide to include frequent reference to the great intellectual challenges of the time. Science, Logic and Philosophy were taught alongside biblical and theological subjects. Encouraged by regular reports of the Academy, members of the churches began to take a keener interest in its work and new students came in larger numbers. A library appeal was launched which was indirectly instrumental in prompting Andrew Gifford to bequeath his valuable collection of books to Bristol. Another tutor was appointed, the three-year course was extended to four and the premises enlarged. For Bristol it was a time of conspicuous growth, and the credit was due to the Evans' initiative in forming the Education Society. The rise of similar societies for the imaginative support of ministerial training was to become characteristic of educational enterprise in other parts of the country.

Early initiatives in theological education usually took the form of personal oversight of a student's training by a leading pastor in whose home the prospective minister came to live. Under this arrangement John Fawcett trained young men in his home at Hebden Bridge and his former pupil, John Sutcliff, received students at Olney. At least thirty-three students studied under Sutcliff's supervision, six of whom went on from Olney for further academic work at Bristol. Sutcliff's academy had, for obvious reasons, a clear missionary commitment and almost a third of its students went to work overseas. Sutcliff's quiet contribution to the denomination's missionary work at home and abroad was considerable. The young shoemaker, William Carey, lived only ten miles away. As an Olney church member he had benefited from Sutcliff's teaching and been guided by him while he was running his own school at Moulton.

In 1804 an event in London enabled some of Sutcliff's Olney students to obtain financial support for their ministerial training. In that year London's Baptist Education Society was revived, largely owing to the initiative of the minister of the Prescot Street church, Abraham Booth (1734-1806). The earlier Society, formed in 1752,[43] had encountered many discouragements and its work been abandoned, but at the beginning of the nineteenth century Booth believed that the time was ripe for a fresh initiative. Largely self-educated, Abraham Booth had begun his ministry within the life of the General Baptist churches. In the course of his travels and wider reading, he came to question the Arminian theology of his General Baptist friends. His first printed work was a poem, 'Absolute Predestination', in which he criticised Calvinistic theology, but further reading convinced him that his initial judgments on the subject had been ill-considered and immature. He found himself happier among the Particular Baptists and eventually wrote a book, *The Reign of Grace* (1768), which was to make considerable impact on those churches. In the year following its publication, he was ordained to the pastorate of Prescot Street and remained there for thirty-eight years. A good deal of London support for the new Missionary Society depended on Booth's advocacy. He was a zealous encourager of William Carey with whom he was in frequent correspondence. In 1796 Carey wrote to Booth from India: 'Your very affectionate letters have been as cordials to my soul'. Booth gave support equally to the establishment of the Home Missionary Society, the launching of Sunday School work and the abolition of the slave-trade. He also recognised the importance of a well-trained ministry. For this reason he enlisted the co-operation of a number of friends in the summer of 1804 and the Baptist Education Society began its new work. [44]

Booth died in 1806, but one of his partners in the enterprise, William Newman (1773-1835) [45] pastor at the Bow church, took up the cause. In 1810 premises in the form of two large houses were opened for an academy at Stepney [46] with Newman as its Principal. Reared in Anglicanism, Newman was converted at the age of ten and worked in his early teens as a junior teacher at John Collett Ryland's school at Enfield. Ryland (1723-92) had formerly served as minister at Warwick, then College Lane, Northampton, and was father of John Ryland, Bristol's Principal. J. C. Ryland was happier in the 'high' Calvinist tradition than was either his son or Newman, but the older Ryland's influence upon Newman was profound, and Newman was an industrious student and scholar, widely read, and a specially gifted linguist. Burdened with the continuing responsibilities of a demanding pastorate at Bow, troubled by poor health and seemingly lacking a necessary sense of humour, Newman's years at the Stepney Academy were not without their difficulties, but the Education Society owed him an incalculable debt.

Leaders in the north of England were equally aware of the need for well-equipped ministers. Baptists in Yorkshire and Lancashire recognised the valuable training supervised by John Fawcett but, as with the Evans partnership in Bristol, additional support was necessary. When, in 1804, Thomas Langdon reminded the Association of the need for educated pastors, interested friends responded by forming the Northern Education Society. Fawcett was a well-respected and able teacher who, when Caleb Evans died in 1792, was invited to succeed him at Bristol. He declined, however, preferring to remain in the north of England. When the new Northern Academy was opened in 1805, Fawcett was sixty-five and a younger man was needed to lead the enterprise. After fruitless invitations to several leaders, including Joseph Kinghorn, James Hinton and Robert Hall,

Jnr, the work eventually fell to William Steadman. Surveying the problems of the north soon after his arrival, he wrote:

> Most of the ministers are illiterate, their talents small, their manner dull and uninteresting, their systems of divinity contracted, their maxims of church discipline rigid, their exertions scarcely any at all. [47]

Steadman combined his new Academy work at Horton with the leadership of the Westgate church in Bradford. It was an exacting responsibility which he shouldered on his own for twelve years, until additional help was provided in the person of Jonathan Edwards Ryland, son of the Bristol Principal. Steadman began his teaching in hired rooms with one student, but gradually the work grew and his example and influence began to have effect. Keenly committed to evangelistic work, he steered the Yorkshire and Lancashire Association's churches into the direction of active itinerancy. The Industrial Revolution was slowly changing the face of the northern counties. Steadman appealed to his fellow Baptists to follow Christ in his compassion for those ignorant of the Christian message. In new industrial communities a crowded mission field was emerging all around the churches:

> Towns and villages are enlarging; new villages as populous as towns in other parts of the kingdom are springing up, until the whole country is, as it were, overspread with habitations. [48]

Steadman reminded the northern churches of the evangelistic success of leaders in the Evangelical Revival, like Whitefield, Wesley and Grimshaw, and pleaded with his contemporaries to respond to the challenge with similar enthusiasm. His students were enlisted in the growing work, many hundreds of people were reached and new churches firmly established. The young man who had travelled with Saffery throughout Cornwall preaching the good news maintained his zeal until the end of his days. In 1825, immediately following his retirement, he wrote the Association's Circular Letter, still reminding his many friends of their obligation 'to promote the spread of the Gospel, and to establish new churches within the limits of the Association'. [49] When Steadman undertook his initial survey of the northern counties he went, among other places, to Manchester and was urged to settle in the pastorate there and make that growing industrial centre the home of the new Academy. Manchester was the largest of the places he had visited, and several of the Education Society's most generous supporters were living there, but Steadman decided to settle in Bradford while the Manchester pastoral vacancy was filled by a high Calvinist minister, William Gadsby.[50]

Controversy

The co-operative evangelistic enterprises we have described were rooted in the Calvinism typical of Fuller's writings. In 1805, the year the northern counties opened their Academy, Gadsby took his Manchester church out of the Yorkshire and Lancashire Association. He was decidedly unhappy about current trends, like theological colleges, association enterprises and itinerant preaching.[51] Fiercely opposed to Fullerism,[52] this magnetic preacher had extraordinary success in reaching working-class people with his rugged but logical message, attractively spiced with natural wit and humour. Several of his converts naturally found themselves led into the ministry and, influenced by his teaching, kept their churches away from the developing partnership of the Particular Baptist associations.

In East Anglia other leaders were equally resistant to new movements. The Norfolk and Suffolk Association had established its corporate life in 1769 on the basis of closed or strict Communion; only believers baptised by immersion were free to partake of the Lord's Supper. Suffolk's oldest Baptist church (Bildeston) was excluded from the fellowship of the association because it did not restrict admission to the Table as the association required.[53] The Wattisfield Independent minister, Thomas Harmer, made the observation in 1774 that the association's 'assemblies carry their notions very high which, it is presumed, is the reason why several other churches are not associated with them'.[54] Considerable evangelistic activity appears to have taken place alongside this exclusivist communion policy: Charles Farmery of Diss and John Thompson of Grundisburgh are two who made their churches centres of vibrant witness to the surrounding villages, resulting in the establishment of new congregations. In eleven years at Diss, Farmery baptised nearly three hundred people, while in a similar period Thompson baptised almost five hundred. But in 1806 some churches in the association expressed their concern about the moderate Calvinism which often prompted evangelistic outreach of this kind. It was argued that a 'Testimony' ought to be drawn up opposing Fuller's teaching and this was done and officially adopted the following year. It was maintained that Fullerism 'tended covertly to introduce the Arminian doctrine of general redemption'.[55] The association's decision foreshadowed a cleavage which took place twenty-four years later when a New Association was formed consisting of those churches which insisted on the necessity of believers' baptism 'as a pre-requisite to the Lord's Supper' - now known as 'Strict Baptists'. By that time the matter of open and closed communion had caused further division and amongst people with firmly held convictions on both sides some breach of fellowship was inevitable.

This East Anglian Communion controversy has a wider historical background. John Bunyan had insisted that believers' baptism should not be made a condition for participation at the Lord's Supper, though his 'open-communion' views were strenuously opposed by men like William Kiffin and most of his Baptist contemporaries. The issue was debated afresh in the second half of the eighteenth century. Daniel Turner of Abingdon maintained that the Lord's Table must be kept open to all 'who appear to love our Lord Jesus Christ in sincerity'. His influence can be clearly seen in the covenant of the Oxford (New Road) church which stated that its members could 'find no warrant in the word of God' to make any 'difference of sentiment' about infant or believers' baptism 'any bar to communion at the Lord's Table in particular, or to church fellowship in general'. Turner's 'open-communion' convictions were shared by other leading ministers such as John Collett Ryland, Robert Robinson and John Ryland, but there were others like Abraham Booth who were offended by what Turner and Ryland, Snr, had written in their pseudonymous tract, *A Modest Plea for Free Communion at the Lord's Table*. Booth and Fuller insisted that only those who had been baptised as believers should be permitted to share in the Lord's Supper.

In the second decade of the nineteenth century this highly controversial topic was given renewed expression in the pamphlets written by Joseph Kinghorn, an intellectually formidable advocate of the 'Strict Communion' position, and Robert Hall, Jnr, the new and vigorous champion of the unrestricted 'Bunyan' view. The future was with the advocates of Hall's outlook. Inevitably, in an environment where regular attendance at the Lord's Supper implied commitment to the local fellowship, 'open communion' convictions became the first step to 'open membership'.[56]

Union

Although there were issues to divide the Particular Baptists in the opening decade of the century, there was far more to unite them. The revived life of associations and the circulation of their printed letters,[57] the formation of Missionary Societies at home and abroad, the widespread promotion of denominational interest between 1790 and 1802 through John Rippon's *Baptist Annual Register,* and the appearance from 1809 onwards of the *Baptist Magazine,* with its more frequent exchange of information, all served to heighten the Particular Baptist sense of identity. On a summer morning in 1812 over sixty ministers met in Rippon's Carter Lane church to discuss the possibility of a national network of Particular Baptist churches. They came to agree that 'a more general Union of the Particular (or Calvinistic) Baptist churches in the United Kingdom is very desirable'[58] and churches and associations were encouraged to send their representatives to a meeting the following June. That initial meeting on 25th June 1812 had been reminded that a more unified denominational life would be advantageous in view of the needs of the Missionary Society for realistic home support. There were also other features of Baptist life which would benefit from a more closely integrated denominational structure. New academies had been formed, which were looking for practical co-operation, financial help and the partnership of churches outside their immediate neighbourhood. In view of England's rapidly changing industrial scene, itinerant evangelism was in need of organisation on a more united basis and not left entirely to local initiative, useful in places as this had been. The developing Sunday School movement would be enriched by mutual conversation about the best methods and schemes to increase its effectiveness. New congregations would soon be in need of adequate buildings to accommodate their growing numbers and some of these churches would be encouraged if monetary help might occasionally be forthcoming from a wider constituency. Social needs had also become apparent, including the provision of necessary education for children of deceased ministers. An annual meeting of church representatives from all over the country could give itself to discussion and action on many of these urgent topics. Rippon served the venture as a respected elder statesman, but a key worker in the project was Joseph Ivimey (1773-1834) who had published an important article in the *Baptist Magazine* for June 1811 under the title, 'Union Essential to Prosperity'; it certainly helped to prepare the ground for the formation of the General Union. The inauguration of a national pattern of assembly life was no mean achievement of that particular time. Not every minister shared the enthusiasm of Rippon, Ivimey and their colleagues. Fuller was very sceptical initially, highly suspicious of any movement which was dominated by London, and he was not alone. More seriously, the political context of the times hardly encouraged the formation of new structures. England was at war with France and in some people's eyes Nonconformists had been far too outspoken about liberty. The quest for religious and political freedom was an important aspect of witness in this period and one that was by no means without opponents.

Freedom

The formation of associations, and the vigorous itinerancy which became characteristic of Baptists as well as of other Nonconformists at this time, gave offence to those already uneasy about dissent. It was one thing for Nonconformity to stay within the narrow confines of their meeting-houses; it was something quite different when they adopted a propagandist spirit[59] and set about establishing new communities of dissenters in parishes where the Established Church had been without a serious rival for decades. It was the conviction of some that severe limits ought to be placed upon Nonconformity. Could even its patriotism be taken for granted?[60]

In the closing decades of the eighteenth century it was widely known that in the War of American Independence the sympathies of most dissenters were with the colonists.[61] In 1773, immediately prior to the outbreak of the war, Benjamin Franklin went so far as to claim: 'The dissenters are all for us'.[62] The fact that Robert Hall, Snr, used three shillings of his limited income in 1775 to buy two books on 'American matters' suggests that Baptists were eager to learn about the colonists' cause.[63] Later, when John Rippon reflected on the issue, he wrote: 'I believe that all our Baptist ministers in town except two, and most of our brethren in the country, were on the side of the Americans in the late dispute ... We believe that the independence of America will for a while secure the liberty of this country'.[64] Rippon's qualification, 'for a while', is noteworthy. Dissenters felt unable to take their partial freedom for granted. They were always under suspicion and it was important for them constantly to be on the alert concerning their religious liberty.

In the 1770s some Baptists feared that distinctive nonconformist principles, with their ideal of freedom, were in danger or neglect. The Cambridge minister, Robert Robinson, told the newly-formed (and short-lived) Eastern Association in 1776 that 'while we were zealous in maintaining the doctrine, and morality of the gospel, we should also take pains to inculcate the grounds and reasons of our dissent from the established hierarchy'.[65]

The Association invited Robinson to draw up a scheme of popular lectures which was published in 1778 under the title, *A Plan of Lectures on the Principles of Nonconformity. For the Instruction of Catechumens*. Robinson's insistence on clear instruction regarding the principles of dissent was given national publicity and his book provoked adverse comment in Parliament from both Pitt and Burke. In the course of a 1787 debate on the repeal of the Test and Corporation Acts, Pitt said that there were some dissenters 'who would not allow that any establishment was necessary ... they were a class of dissenters in Cambridgeshire' and he then named 'the Minister of the Congregation, Mr Robinson'.[66] In 1790 Burke referred to 'printed catechisms' in use among 'young nonconformists' and maintained that that 'written by Mr Robinson ... consisted of one continued invective against kings and bishops ... In short, it was a catechism of misanthropy, a catechism of anarchy, a catechism of confusion'.[67]

Burke's irritation, and that of others, was due in part to widespread fear that dissenters were sympathetic to the French Revolution.[68] He continued his speech by making direct reference to the troubles in France. Burke was convinced that publications such as Robinson's catechism, if widely used among dissenters, could produce for the established Church

> a rising generation of its determined enemies, while, possibly, the dissenting preachers were themselves recommending the same sort of robbery and plunder of the wealth of the Church as has happened in France.[69]

Richard Price, an Arian minister who had taken a leading part in supporting the colonists' view during the American war, confirmed Burke's worst suspicions regarding dissenters when, in 1789, he expressed his pleasure that the French people were at last 'breaking their fetters, and claiming justice from their oppressors'.[70]

Burke replied with his famous and forceful *Reflections on the Revolution in France* (1790). In that year Robert Robinson died, but similar views about freedom were given forceful expression by his successor in the Cambridge pastorate, Robert Hall (the gifted son of Robert Hall, Snr, of Arnesby) who, in the course of his ministry at Cambridge, Leicester and Bristol, became widely recognised as one of the most outstanding preachers in England. Throughout his life he constantly battled against poor health, but his moral and spiritual vigour was unlimited. In 1791 John Clayton, the Congregational minister of London's fashionable King's Weigh House Chapel, published a pamphlet entitled *The Duty of Christians to Magistrates* in which he urged dissenting ministers not to preach on political issues. Hall considered Clayton's directives 'absurd' and went on to insist that Christianity 'instead of weakening our attachment to the principles of freedom, or withdrawing them from our attention, renders them doubly dear to us, by giving us an interest in them proportioned to the value of those religious privileges which they secure and protect'. In the course of his argument Hall does nothing to conceal where his sympathies lie on the French situation. In vindicating 'the revolution in France', he maintains that it

> may be defended upon its *principles* against the friends of arbitrary power, by displaying the value of freedom, the equal rights of mankind, the folly and injustice of those regal or aristocratic pretensions by which those rights were invaded; accordingly, in this light it has been justified with the utmost success.[71]

News of serious disorders in revolutionary France, with its gruesome stories of bloodshed and anarchy, naturally reduced the support for the rebels' cause. But, even with the execution of the French king in January 1793 and the declaration of war the following month, some Baptists were cautious about identifying with the general uproar. They did not approve of the revolution's methods, but they fully sympathised with its aims. When, in March of that year, England was called to 'a general Fast', Joseph Kinghorn, the Norwich Particular Baptist minister, asked: 'Can we wish the destruction of a people who have just risen from slavery and on whose existence perhaps the freedom of Europe depends? ... Would not their destruction effectually rivet the chains on ourselves?'[72] Two months later Robert Hall was writing to Kinghorn to enlist his help in securing a Norwich bookseller who would take copies of Hall's new book, *An Apology for the Freedom of the Press and for General Liberty*. Its author insisted that there was nothing remotely violent in the pamphlet and Kinghorn made a point of ordering copies for distribution. Eventually, continuing news of cruelties inflicted by atheistic revolutionaries compelled Kinghorn to express the disillusionment felt by many: 'All those notions of liberty which the French Revolution very generally raised a few years ago are at an end, they are the tyrants not the deliverers of men'.[73]

It can certainly be argued that, as far as dissenters were concerned, the American Declaration of Independence articulated the ideal of freedom and provided an incentive for renewed vigour in the pursuit of civil and religious liberty. It is also likely that the campaign suffered a serious setback in England because of what happened in France, and it was not until hostilities were over that toleration came with the 1828 repeal of the Test and Corporation Acts. It needs to be realised that the constant pursuit of religious liberty was an item in the Nonconformist creed which could never be divorced from its evangelistic concern. It was not the case that Hall had one message and Fuller another. When Carey wrote his famous *Enquiry* he made the links unmistakably clear:

> we have within these few years been favoured with some tokens for good ... I trust our *monthly prayer meetings* for the success of the gospel have not been in vain ... yea a glorious door is opened, and is likely to be opened wider and wider, by the spread of civil and religious liberty.[74]

Any fear that the limited freedom they enjoyed was precariously held was soon justified. At the height of the conflict with France, Lord Sidmouth introduced his abortive bill (1811) against unlicensed preachers. Although this was aimed primarily at the Methodists, it was a serious danger to itinerancy and lay preaching within any denomination. Sidmouth maintained that it

> was a matter of importance to society, that not every person, without regard to his moral character or his intellectual faculties, should assume to himself the office of instructing his fellow-creatures in their duty to God.

Although not deliberately offensive in the way that he made his point, Sidmouth was disturbed that among those who were applying for licences to preach were 'cobblers, tailors, pig-drovers and chimney-sweepers'. In opposing the proposed legislation, Lord Holland expressed regret that his fellow-peer 'had spoken invidiously of persons in inferior situations of life becoming preachers, for surely they were fully entitled to preach those religious opinions which they conscientiously believed'.[75] If cobblers had earlier been denied the privilege, William Carey would have been silenced. In Baptist churches throughout the country there were many like him who treasured freedom and evangelism as inseparable partners. They knew that if robbed of one it might only be a matter of time before they lost the other. The 'glorious door' must be kept open.

Partners

The closely related interests of mission and freedom were not the exclusive concern of Baptists. The common pursuit of civil equality provided the 'three denominations' with natural occasions for meeting throughout the eighteenth century.[76] Sidmouth's Bill threatened evangelistic initiatives at local level, and Methodists came alongside dissenters in the quest for religious liberty.[77] Moreover, it was not a selfish campaign; nonconformists were unitedly concerned about intolerance abroad as well as restrictions at home.[78] The anti-slave movement had also encouraged interdenominational co-operation, as when the Bristol tutor, Joseph Hughes (1769-1833) , identified with some of the city's Anglicans, Quakers, Baptists and others in local work for abolition.[79] Itinerancy also served to further local relationships between Baptist preachers and members of other Communions. Shortly after moving from Bristol to his Battersea pastorate, Hughes was instrumental in forming the Surrey Mission Society (1798), a joint initiative by Independents and Baptists to sponsor evangelistic preaching in 'the dark villages of the county'.[80] Baptist itinerants frequently observed that their paedobaptist friends were equally concerned about Christian witness in rural communities. During their West Country journeys Steadman and Saffery were pleased to discover how closely they could work with other Christians, whatever their denominational allegiance. Methodists and Independents lent their meeting-houses, gave additional practical help and treated the visiting ministers 'with great kindness and affection'.[81] There were times when evangelical Anglicans listened appreciatively to their preaching and offered them warm encouragement.[82]

The decades which spanned the eighteenth and nineteenth centuries saw the rise of an astonishing number of new societies. The medical, religious, moral and educational charities formed between 1780 and 1800 more than trebled the number which commenced their work during the previous twenty years, while those founded between the turn of the century and 1820 rose to almost twice the number of the preceding two decades. [83] Christian societies and specialist agencies were quickly established to meet the challenge of new opportunities and Baptists played a significant part in many of them.

The rapidly developing Sunday School movement was, initially, in several places, an ambitious venture in ecumenical co-operation. The new Sunday Schools needed expert guidance, free text books and extra financial support. Constructive propaganda was also necessary. In the light of disturbing news from France, potential donors had to be reassured that educating the poor was not a sinister, pro-revolutionary exercise. [84] All these worthwhile assignments became the responsibility of the first of several national Sunday School organisations, the Sunday School Society, founded in 1785 mainly through the efforts of a Baptist layman, William Fox, [85] a deacon at Abraham Booth's church and a friend of Robert Raikes. The new Society was, like many others, ecumenical from the start, its committee members drawn equally from Church and Dissent.

The early eighteenth century charity schools had been small by comparison, serving at most 20-25 children, but these schools were much larger; those aided by the new Sunday School Society were attracting between 90 and 100 scholars. [86] Imaginative help was certainly needed. In the year prior to the society's foundation, Wesley preached in Bingley and recorded in his *Journal* that he saw 250 children in their recently-formed Sunday School: 'I find these schools springing up wherever I go ... Who knows but some of these schools may become nurseries for Christians'. [87]

Baptist preachers had similar ambitions for the new movement. They pointed out that the 'uncultivated land' [88] of the child's mind had enormous potential and that today's child is tomorrow's citizen. A good Christian education is a rich investment in a better society. [89] The London, Maze Pond, minister, James Dore, preached on behalf of the Sunday School Society, believing that these schools had immense evangelistic opportunities:

> The Bible is the gift of God to men in general ... The poor and unlearned are as much entitled to the Book as the rich and learned ... Christ came to save all men. [90]

With increasing literacy, tracts, pamphlets and modestly-priced books were urgently necessary to make the Christian message more widely known. Joseph Hughes of Battersea and the Stepney Principal, William Newman, were among the founding fathers of the Religious Tract Society (1799), and Hughes became the Society's first Secretary.[91] It was at one of the Society's committee meetings that a Calvinistic Methodist minister, Thomas Charles of Bala, asked 'if a large and cheap edition of the Bible could be had in Welsh', which led Hughes to ask whether 'a society might be formed for the purpose; and if for Wales, why not for the kingdom; why not for the whole world?'[92] The challenge led to the establishment of the British and Foreign Bible Society (1804) which Hughes also served as Secretary from its inception until his death almost thirty years later. Baptist involvement in the new evangelical societies was certainly not peripheral.

Hughes valued his friendship with evangelical leaders of other denominations such as William Jay of Bath, Hannah More, William Wilberforce and other members of the nearby 'Clapham Sect'.[93] His ecumenism was not simply a useful device to promote and further educational and philanthropic activities; it eagerly anticipated mutually acceptable ministry in the local churches with opportunities for shared worship:

> I long to see the day in which Episcopalians, Presbyterians, Methodists, Independents, and Baptists will exchange pulpits, and meet at the same sacramental board.[94]

The active pursuit of missionary ideas encouraged many people to cross denominational frontiers. Samuel Pearce wrote home to his wife from London in September 1795, enthusiastically reporting David Bogue's famous sermon in which the preacher condemned denominational rivalry and rejoiced in 'the funeral of bigotry'. Bogue's sermon was preached at the inauguration of what later became known as the London Missionary Society, and Pearce gave this new interdenominational enterprise his immediate financial support.[95] Similarly, other Particular Baptist leaders like Fuller, James Hinton, John Ryland, and Robert Hall, Jnr, shared in the work of the London Society for promoting Christianity amongst the Jews (1809),[96] another venture in missionary collaboration.

When Carey wrote his *Enquiry* (1792) he was sure that, 'in the present divided state of Christendom', overseas missions were best launched by each denomination 'engaging separately in the work'[97] but a decade later he realised how valuable it would be if the churches could work closer together. He longed that it might be possible to have 'a general association of all denominations of Christians, from the four quarters of the world' and dared to hope that this meeting might be held in 1810, or 1812 at the latest. Carey told Fuller that he did not doubt that such a conference 'would be attended with very important effects; we could understand one another better, and more entirely enter into one another's views by two hours conversation than by two or three years epistolary correspondence'.[98] It was an ambitious dream, not fulfilled until a century later at the Edinburgh Missionary Conference (1910), but Carey's enthusiasm for missions had served to make Christians of differing ecclesiastical allegiance more deeply aware of their inter-dependence. Pearce wrote to tell Carey that the founders of the London Missionary Society

> publicly owned that *our* zeal kindled theirs, and it was God who first touched *your* heart with fire from his holy altar! To him be all the praise.[99]

Samuel Pearce gladly acknowledged his own debt to other Christians. His love for missions was first inspired by a Methodist sermon. It was frequently encouraged by the enthusiasm of Edward Williams, a neighbouring Independent minister, and challenged by news of Moravians working in Greenland.[100] No denomination had a monopoly of truth, spirituality or vision. As zealous collectors for the Particular Baptist Missionary Society, Andrew Fuller and William Crabtree[101] were not alone in inviting regular subscriptions from Anglican vicars and curates; people with generous minds were only too glad to share in such an influential work, by whatever name it was called.

During the eighteenth century, the Evangelical Revival had, in many places, broken through local Baptist insularity. Several of the denomination's leaders had been brought to personal faith through the ministry of a preacher from another tradition. ·Not infrequently, the itinerant preaching of evangelical Anglicans, like Grimshaw in Yorkshire and John Berridge in the eastern counties, had led to the establishment of a local Baptist church.[102] Moderate Calvinism provided evangelicals with a unifying and highly articulate, theological identity as well as fresh motivation for mission. Distinctive denominational convictions were no longer regarded as insuperable barriers to fellowship and service. Churchmen and dissenters sang each other's hymns,[103] drew inspiration from one another's books[104] and even preached each other's sermons. When the Baptists at Whitchurch, Hampshire, were without a preacher on either Sundays or weeknights they publicly read a sermon by John Newton, vicar of St Mary Woolnoth, and wrote to tell him so, hoping that one day he would come to preach to them in person.[105]

It is not always remembered that, in the first instance, association letters were frequently used to encourage the Particular Baptist people to look beyond their denominational frontiers. In 1779, long before the birth of the pan-evangelical societies, the Midland Association was urging its members to remember that 'our love is not to be confined with the narrow limits of a party, but extended to all that bear the image of Christ, of whatever denomination'.[106]

The year before their own Missionary Society came into being, the Particular Baptist ministers of Yorkshire and Lancashire condemned that 'odious demon' of religious bigotry 'which frequently appears under the disguise of a zeal for truth'. That Christians, they said,

> differ in their sentiments respecting some of the speculative doctrines of theology, and some of the external modes of religous worship, is not at all to be wondered at; but that they should be so ready to censure and condemn one another on this account, is truly astonishing. There is such a difference in the capacities, education, circumstances and connections of men that it would be unreasonable to expect that their religious opinions should be exactly alike ... When the apostle exhorts us to be 'of the same mind and of the same judgment' he does not so much intend a unity of opinion as a unity of affection.

In language strongly reminiscent of the earlier Midland letter, these northern congregations were reminded that the genuine Christian 'will not confine his affections within the narrow limits of a party'. He will feel 'an affectionate regard for all good men, by whatever denomination they may be distinguished'.[107]

At the close of our period it was not only General and Particular Baptists who were drawn closer together in the pursuit of common ideals. Local initiatives presented wider opportunities for mutual help and united witness. Particular Baptists in Bedfordshire, of both 'open' and 'closed' communion convictions, joined with Anglicans, Methodists,

Moravians and Independents in responding to Samuel Greatheed's appeal for a 'union of Christians' in their county.[108] The new century provided Baptist people with further engagement in ecumenical partnership as well as denominational integration.[109] Denominational horizons continued to be extended to include all who loved Christ.

In the course of his West Country itinerancy, William Steadman occasionally met Christians of a different spirit. One in particular provided him with hospitality but would rather have enticed him into a divisive argument than identify with his evangelistic preaching: 'Plagued with the impertinence and bigotry of my host', he writes in his journal, 'who would lug me into a dispute about baptism'.[110] But, convinced Baptist that he was, the guest treasured a higher loyalty: 'Still find I love those who love Jesus Christ, though they do not follow in all things with me'.

It was in this context that Steadman's son and biographer quoted the saying of one of Carey's partners, John Chamberlain, a pioneer missionary in North India: 'I am content to be a Baptist, but glory in being a Christian'.[111] Motivated by love, such men knew that grace insists on wide horizons.

* * * * * * * *

NOTES AND REFERENCES

Abbreviations used

B.A.R. I,II,III,IV	John Rippon, *The Baptist Annual Register,* I (1790–93), II (1794–7), III (1798–1801), IV (1801–2)
B.Q.	*Baptist Quarterly*
Crosby I,II,III,IV	Thomas Crosby, *The History of the English Baptists,* 4 vols, 1738–40
D.N.B.	*Dictionary of National Biography*
Ivimey I,II,III,IV	Joseph Ivimey, *History of the English Baptists,* 4 vols, 1811–30
M.G.A. I,II	W. T. Whitley (ed.), *Minutes of the General Assembly of General Baptists,* 2 vols, 1909–10
Taylor I,II	Adam Taylor, *History of the English General Baptists,* 2 vols, 1818
T.B.H.S.	*Transactions of the Baptist Historical Society*
Wood	J. H. Wood, *A Condensed History of the General Baptists of the New Connexion...,* 1847

Where no place of publication is given, London should be
assumed. The spelling and punctuation of the quotations
have been modernised.

Chapter 1 : 'Expectation of great things'

1   Gilbert Burnet, *The History of my Own Times*, Oxford 1833, Vol.IV, Book VI, 550.

2   Ibid., Vol.IV, Book VI, 550; Vol.IV, Book V, 1-2.

3   G. V. Bennett, *The Tory Crisis in Church and State 1688-1703*, 1975, 12-13.

4   G. Burnet, op.cit., Vol.IV, Book V, 21.

5   Joseph Jenkins, *A sermon preached on the 22nd March 1702 upon ... the death of ... William III*, 1702.

6   Barry Coward, *The Stuart Age*, 1980, 349.

7   Geoffrey Holmes (ed.), *Britain after the Glorious Revolution 1689-1714*, 1969, 167. For further reference to occasional conformity, see Chapter 3 below.

8   [Samuel Wesley], *A Letter from a Country Divine to his Friend in London concerning the education of the Dissenters in their Private Academies in several parts of this nation*, 1703, 6-7.

9   Philip Doddridge, *Charge preached at the Ordination of the Rev. Abraham Tozer*, 1745, 53-54.

10   Benjamin Stinton, *A Discourse of Divine Providence*, 2nd edn, 1714, 25-6.

11   Dr John Taylor of Norwich, for example, held that Catholicism, 'an astonishing apostasy', and an 'idolatrous church, the mother of harlots', was a 'monstrous and most audacious corruption' of Christianity (Richard Watson (ed.), *A Collection of Theological Tracts*, Cambridge 1785, Vol.III, 313). In 1762 William Warburton, Bishop of Gloucester, wrote: 'I have always regarded Popery rather as an impious and impudent combination against the sense and rights of mankind, than as a species of religion' (W. S. Taylor and J. H. Pringle (ed.), *Correspondence of William Pitt, Earl of Chatham*, 1838, Vol.II, 191).

12   See Edward F. Carpenter, *Thomas Tenison, Archbishop of Canterbury: His Life and Times*, 1948, 35-68, for an account of anti-Roman anxiety in the reign of James II; cf. J. R. Jones, *Country and Court 1658-1744*, 1978, 197-202.

13   John Piggott, *Eleven Sermons*, 1714, 132; cf. William Wake, *A Sermon preached in the Parish Church of St James Westminster April 16th 1696*, 1696, 10.

14   Piggott, *Eleven Sermons*, 21.

15   See, for example, Robert Robinson, *The Miscellaneous Works of Robert Robinson,* Harlow 1807, Vol.III, 184, Andrew Gunton Fuller, *The Complete Works of Andrew Fuller,* 1841, 451, 453, 464, Olinthus Gregory (ed.), *The Works of Robert Hall,* 1841, Vol.IV, 241-61, 393-5. *The Western Association Letter of 1780* grieves that 'because of the alarming growth of Popery, the Gospel of Christ is neglected'.

16   William Bisset, *Plain English: A Sermon preached at St Mary-le-Bow ... for Reformation of Manners,* 1704,19.

17   Whitelocke Bulstrode, *The Charge ... to the Grand Jury and other Juries,* 1718, 35.

18   G. Burnet, op.cit., Vol.IV, Book V, 176-7.

19   M. H. Lee (ed.), *Diaries and Letters of Philip Henry,* 1882, 193.

20   For example, Benjamin Stinton, *A Sermon Preached the 27th November 1713 in commemoration of the Great and Dreadful Storm in November 1703,* 3rd edn, 1714; Andrew Gifford, *A Sermon in commemoration of the Great Storm commonly called the High Wind (1703) ... with an account of the damage done by it,* 1733.

21   Benjamin Keach, *A Golden Mine Opened,* 1694, 5.

22   *His Majesties Letter to the Lord Bishop of London,* 1689, 4.

23   Thomas Tenison, *His Grace the Lord Archbishop of Canterbury's Letter to the Right Reverend the Lord Bishops of his Province,* 1699, 1.

24   Thomas Bisse, *Pride and Ignorance the Ground of Errors in Religion,* 1716, 26, where that outlook is strenuously opposed.

25   Alexander Pope, *An Essay on Man,* Epistle iii, 305-6.

26   John Piggott, op.cit., 328-9, 289-90, 295, 287.

27   P. Rehakosht, *A Plain and Just Account of a most Horrid and Dismal Plague began at Rowel, alias Rothwell,* 1692, with its derogatory reference to the preaching of 'shoemakers, joiners, dyers, tailors, weavers, farmers', and Peter Toon, *The Emergence of Hyper-Calvinism in English Nonconformity 1689-1765,* 1967, 64.

28   E. N. Williams, *A Documentary History of England,*

Harmondsworth 1965, Vol.ii, 116.

29   G. Burnet, op.cit., Book VI, Vol.IV, 394.

30   G. F. Nuttall, *Calendar of the Correspondence of Philip Doddridge DD (1704-1751)*, 1979, Letters 1173, 1460, 1539, 1742-3.

31   Roy Porter, *English Society in the Eighteenth Century*, Harmondsworth 1982, 31.

32   Alan Everitt, 'Nonconformity in Country Parishes' in Joan Thirsk, *Land, Church and People: Essays presented to Professor H. P. R. Finberg*, Reading 1970, 186. For further comment on the geographic distribution of dissent, see Michael Watts, *The Dissenters*, Oxford 1978, Vol.I, 267-89.

33   G. F. Nuttall, 'Letters by Benjamin Francis', *Trafodion*, Cymdeithas Hanes Bedyddwyr Cymru 1983, 6.

34   Ibid., 7-8.

35   G. Burnet, op.cit., Vol.IV, Book V, 1.

36   Song of Solomon 4.12, cf. Matthias Maurice, *Monuments of Mercy*, 1729, Epistle Dedicatory: 'You are a Garden enclosed, and I earnestly desire you may be such a well watered one, that Plants of Renown may spring up, flourish and fructify among you'.

Chapter 2 : 'Against clear light'

1   Thomas Grantham, *Christianismus Primitivus*, 1678, Conclusion to Book IV, Chapter 3, Section IV, 211-2.

2   *M.G.A.*, I, 26-8.

3   For Smyth's Gainsborough connections see Michael Watts, *The Dissenters: From the Reformation to the French Revolution*, Oxford 1978, 282, and A. de M. Chesterman, *Axholme Baptists*, Crowle, Lincs., 1949, 9-10; note also the likely presence of Arminians among the 200 Dutch families which settled in the Isle of Axholme in the early seventeenth century, cf. G. F. Nuttall, *The Puritan Spirit*, 1967, 74, and A. de M. Chesterman, op.cit., 15-16. For the Lollard ancestry of the Home Counties' members, see Arnold H. J. Baines, 'Signatories to the Orthodox Confession, 1679', *B.Q.* XVII, 35-6.

4   Emily Kensett, *History of the Free Christian Church, Horsham, 1721-1921,* Horsham 1921, 10-12; *B.Q.,* I, 81.

5   T. Abbe and H. E. Howson, *Robert Colgate the Immigrant,* New Haven, Conn. 1941, 22.

6   E. B. Underhill, *Records of the Churches of Christ, gathered at Fenstanton, Warboys and Hexham, 1644-1720,* 1854, 45,60,82.

7   Walter Wilson, *The History and Antiquities of Dissenting Churches and Meeting Houses in London, Westminister and Southwark,* 1810, Vol.III, 388-91.

8   *M.G.A.,* I, 60.

9   E. B. Underhill, op.cit., 36-7, 69, 136.

10 Taylor, I, 453.

11 *M.G.A.,* I, 143.

12 G. F. Nuttall, *Calendar,* Letter 254, cf. Edmund Calamy, *A Historical Account of My Own Life,* 1830, I, 159: 'I told him, "he wronged the English Dissenters if he apprehended the generality of them were against the Lord's Prayer ... many among the present Dissenters did use it generally and others frequently".'

13 *M.G.A.,* I, 85.

14 Ibid., 23.

15 L. G. Champion (ed.), *The General Baptist Church of Berkhamsted, Chesham and Tring 1712-1781,* Baptist Historical Society 1985, 18. cf. also 19, 20, 27, 32, 57, 63, 80, 82-3, 97.

16 *M.G.A.,* I, 93-4.

17 Ibid., 135-6.

18 *M.G.A.,* II, 74.

19 Bishop Richard Watson of Llandaff, for example: 'we do not object to the doctrine of the Trinity because it is above our reason, and we cannot apprehend it; but we object to it because we cannot find that it is either literally contained in any passage of Holy Writ, or ca by sound criticism be deduced from it'. (Richard Watson, *Miscellaneous Tracts on Religious, Political, and Agricultural Subjects,* 1815, II, 108).

20   W. L. Lumpkin, *Baptist Confessions of Faith,* Chicago 1959, 295-334.

21   *M.G.A.,* I, 39-40.

22   *M.G.A.,* I, 43.

23   Ibid., 51. For details of the relationship between the two bodies, see Taylor I, 470-80.

24   London dissenting ministers met at Salters' Hall in 1719 to discuss the matter of subscribing to the doctrine of the Trinity and decided by a narrow majority that subscription was not required; see [W. T. Whitley], 'Salters' Hall 1719 and the Baptists', T.B.H.S.,V, 172-189; C. G. Bolam, J. Goring et al., *The English Presbyterians,* 1968, 151-174.

25   *M.G.A.,* I, 40-2.

26   Ibid., 84-5.

27   Ibid., 42.

28   Ibid., 104.

29   Ibid., 108.

30   B. R. White, 'The Baptists of Reading 1652-1715', *B.Q.,* XXII, 255-6.

31   B. R. White, *English Baptists of the Seventeenth Century,* Baptist Historical Society 1983, 14-5, and B. R. White, 'Thomas Crosby, Baptist Historian', *B.Q.,* XXII, 154-68, 219-34.

32   Ivimey, III, 111-2.

33   Crosby, IV, 109-10.

34   Ivimey, III, 152; T. F. Valentine, *Concern for the Ministry,* Teddington, Middlesex [1967], 20-1.

35   L. G. Champion (ed.), op.cit., 32.

36   *M.G.A.,* I, 52-3.

37   Ibid., 68-9. Cf. also the Ford, Bucks, members who were disciplined (1721) for 'sitting under the Presbyterian ministry', W. T. Whitley (ed.), *The Church Books of Ford or Cuddington and Amersham ... Bucks,* 1912, 132.

38   Ibid., 71.

39   Ibid., 75.

40   Ibid., 95.

41   Marius D'Assigny, *The Mystery of Anabaptism Unmasked,* 1709, preface. A list of London Baptist preachers and their trades follows the Contents page.

42   *M.G.A.,* I, 110-1.

43   Ibid., 115.

44   Ibid., 50.

45   Hercules Collins, *The Temple Repaired,* 1702, 29; Benjamin Keach, *A Golden Mine Opened,* 1694, 23; Ivimey, I, 595-7.

46   *M.G.A.,* I, 75.

47   Ibid., 125, cf. *M.G.A.,* II, 308.

48   *M.G.A.,* I, 146.

49   Garnett Ryland, *The Baptists of Virginia 1699-1926,* Richmond, Virginia 1955, 1-8.

50   *M.G.A.,* I, 138-9.

51   Ibid., 141.

52   Ibid., 129-30.

53   Ibid., 118.

54   Ibid., 135.

55   Ibid., 149.

Chapter 3 : 'Earnest hopes'

1   Ivimey, I, 478-81.

2   Ibid., I, 480-510, and *B.A.R.,* IV, following the Index.

3   R. Tudur Jones, *Congregationalism in England 1662-1962,* 1962, 111-2.

4   For a reply to Russen's criticisms, see Joseph Stennett, *An Answer to Mr. David Russen's book entitled Fundamentals without a Foundation,* 1704.

5   Crosby, IV, 129-36.

6   Ivimey, I, 527-9.

7   Ibid., I, 534-5.

8   *T.B.H.S.,* III, 190; W. T. Whitley, *Baptists of North*

149

West England, 1913, 77-80; *Bromsgrove Baptist Church Record Book 1670-1715,* Bromsgrove Baptist Church 1974, 51.

9 E. A. Payne, *The Baptists of Berkshire,* 1951, 72.

10 Ivimey, III, 38-9.

11 Crosby, IV, 108-9, and MS in Angus Library, Regent's Park College, Oxford: 'An Account of the Proceedings of the Society of Baptist Ministers in London from 17th August 1714 to 16th August 1736'.

12 Arians were less radical than Socinians. They generally accepted Christ's 'divinity' (in some sense), pre-existence and atonement, while Socinians rejected these concepts.

13 *T.B.H.S.,* V, 96-114, and Arthur J. Payne, 'The Baptist Board', *B.Q.,* I, 321-6.

14 Crosby, IV, 109-10.

15 T. F. Valentine, op.cit., 4-5.

16 Ibid., 8.

17 Ibid, 35-6.

18 Ibid., 16-7; cf. B. R. White, 'John Gill in London, 1719-1729: A Biographical Fragment', *B.Q.,* XXII, 72-91.

19 H. Danvers, *Treatise on Baptism,* 2nd edn, 1674, Supplement, cf. E. A. Payne, 'Baptists and the Laying on of Hands', *B.Q.,* XV, 209.

20 J. K. Parratt, 'An Early Baptist on the Laying on of Hands', *B.Q.,* XXI, 325-7, 320; cf. Benjamin Keach, *Laying on of Hands upon Baptised Believers,* 1698, 58.

21 E. F. Kevan, *London's Oldest Baptist Church,* 1933, 50-1.

22 David Rees, *The Principles of the Christian Religion digested into several articles: being an account of the faith and practice of the Church of Christ, meeting at Limehouse,* 1713.

23 S. J. Price, 'Sidelights from an old minute book', *B.Q.,* V, 93.

24 W. T. Whitley, 'Seventh Day Baptists in England', *B.Q.,* XII, 252-8; E. A. Payne, 'More about Sabbatarian Baptists', *B.Q.,* XIV, 161-6.

25 Isaac Marlow, *The Truth soberly defended,* 1692.

26 Isaac Marlow, *Controversy of Singing brought to an end,* 1696.

27 William Russell, *Some Brief Animadversions on Mr. Allen's Essay,* 1696.

28 Isaac Marlow, *Some Brief Remarks,* 1692, 11-2.

29 Elias Keach, *The Glory and Ornament of a true Gospel-Constituted Church,* 1697, 17.

30 Ivimey, I, 492.

31 John Piggott, op.cit., 239.

32 Hercules Collins, op.cit., 3.

33 Ibid., 13.

34 Ibid., 17.

35 Joseph Stennett, *Works,* 1732, I, 32 ('Some account of the life of ... Joseph Stennett').

36 Edmund Calamy, *An Account ...,* *1713,* II, Part II, 610.

37 Norman S. Moon, *Education for Ministry: Bristol Baptist College 1679-1979,* Bristol 1979, 3.

38 For Terrill, see Roger Hayden (ed.), *The Records of a Church of Christ in Bristol 1640-1687,* (Bristol Record Society, XXVII), Bristol 1974, 5-11.

39 Norman S. Moon, op.cit., 1-4, and H. Foreman, 'Baptist provision for Ministerial Education in the 18th century', *B.Q.,* XXVII, 358-61.

40 Joseph Stennett, op.cit., 24.

41 Benjamin Keach, *The Gospel Minister's Maintenance Vindicated,* 1689, 1, cf. *B.Q.,* II, 224-31.

42 Benjamin Keach, ibid., 2.

43 Ibid., 3.

44 Ibid., 42.

45 Ibid., 40.

46 Richard Baxter, *Saints Everlasting Rest,* 7th edn, London 1658, Dedication. 'Direction 2' of his 'ten directions'.

47 Benjamin Keach, op.cit., 30-1.

48 Ibid., 72-3.

49 Ibid., 92.

50 J. Stennett, op.cit., I, 9.

51 S. J. Price, 'Dissenting academies 1662-1820', *B.Q.*, VI, 138 and *B.A.R.*, II, 305.

52 B. R. White, 'Thomas Crosby, Baptist Historian', *B.Q.*, XXI, 155; cf. Crosby, I: advertisement following the Appendix.

53 *T.B.H.S.*, IV, 1-32.

54 Crosby, IV, 114-23; cf. M. G. Jones, *The Charity School Movement*, Cambridge 1938, 131-4.

55 Benjamin Keach, *Light broke forth in Wales expelling darkness*, 1696, Dedication to the Paedobaptists.

56 Crosby, IV, 136-7.

57 *The Calendar of Treasury Books January-December 1717*, XXXI, Part I, 46.

58 G. F. Nuttall, *Calendar*, Letters 398, 403, 450.

59 S. J. Price, 'Sidelights from an old minute book', *B.Q.*, V, 87-9; cf. *T.B.H.S.*, V, 122, 223-4, and for its 'very respectable intellectual ancestry', see Christopher Hill, 'Occasional Conformity' in R. B. Knox (ed.), *Reformation, Conformity and Dissent: Essays in honour of Geoffrey Nuttall*, 1977, 199-220.

60 G. F. Nuttall, *The General Body of the Three Denominations: a historical sketch*, 1955.

61 Bernard L. Manning, *The Protestant Dissenting Deputies*, Cambridge 1952, and N. C. Hunt, *Two Early Political Associations*, Oxford 1961.

62 John Piggott, op.cit., 310.

63 Richard Allen, *A Gainful Death, the end of a truly Christian life*, 1700, 40.

Chapter 4 : 'Our unity quite broken'

1 John Hursthouse, *An Epistle to the Baptized Churches in Lincolnshire, together with a Postscript*, Lincoln 1729, quoted in Taylor II, 106-7; see also [Strickland Gough], *An Enquiry into the causes of the Decay of the Dissenting Interest* ... 1730, and similar titles at

this time.

2   *M.G.A.,* II, 52, note.

3   Ibid., 58.

4   Ibid., 67.

5   Ibid., 95-6.

6   Ibid., 49 and note.

7   Ibid., 2.

8   Ibid., 3 note.

9   Ibid., 32.

10   Ibid., 37.

11   Ibid., 32-3.

12   Ibid., 15-16.

13   Ibid., 18.

14   Ibid., 104.

15   Ibid., 33-4.

16   Ibid., 21 note.

17   Ibid., 104; cf. Taylor II, 105.

18   Ibid., 71.

19   Ibid., 14.

20   Ibid., 72-5. It is important to note that there was some variability in General Baptist practice regarding 'marrying out'. In 1736 the Chesham members acknowledged that 'it might be thought justifiable to marry with a sober and pious person though unbaptised' (L. G. Champion, op.cit., 108).

21   Ibid., 7.

22   Ibid,, 19. This fund, established in 1725, was later known as the General Baptist Fund.

23   Ibid., 43-6.

24   Ibid., 48.

25   Ibid., 8.

26   Ibid., 143.

27   Ibid., 7.

28   Ibid., 95-6.

29 Ibid., 102, 104.

30 Ibid., 43.

31 Thomas Brittain, *The Theological Remembrancer,* Northampton 1900, 11, 17, 20.

32 Edwin Welch (ed.), *Two Calvinistic Methodist Chapels 1743-1811: The London Tabernacle and Spa Fields Chapel,* 1975.

33 Thomas Brittain, op.cit., 13.

34 Taylor II, 110.

35 Frank Buffard, *Kent and Sussex Baptist Associations,* Faversham 1963, 40.

36 Taylor II, 2-4.

37 See [Thomas Cook], *Preacher, Pastor, Mechanic: Memoir of the late Mr Samuel Deacon,* Leicester 1888.

38 Percy Austin, 'Barton in the Beans', *B.Q.,* XI, 417-22, and Wood, 157-73.

39 See Frank Beckwith, 'Dan Taylor (1738-1816) and Yorkshire Baptist life', *B.Q.,* IX, 297-306; Adam Taylor, *Memoirs of the Rev. Dan Taylor,* 1820, and *D.N.B.*

40 *M.G.A.,* II, 141.

41 W. T. Whitley, 'The Influence of Whitefield on Baptists', *B.Q.,* V, 36.

42 Gilbert Boyce, *A candid and friendly reply to Mr Dan Taylor's 'A dissertation on singing in the worship of God',* 1787. Taylor's work, published in 1786, was a reply to an earlier Boyce criticism of hymn-singing, *Serious thoughts on the present mode and practice of singing in the public worship of God,* 1785.

Chapter 5 : 'Open for Everyone'

1 Crosby IV, 352-3.

2 MS. 'Records of the Baptist Western Association: 1733-1809' (an address by Caleb Evans) at Bristol Baptist College; cf. J. G. Fuller, *A Brief History of the Western Association,* Bristol 1843, 32.

3 For Brine see Peter Toon, op.cit., 96-103.

4   For the origins and development of high Calvinism see Alan P. F. Sell, *The Great Debate: Calvinism, Arminianism and Salvation,* Worthing 1982, especially chapters 2-3.

5   A. G. Matthews, *Diary of a Cambridge Minister,* Cambridge 1937; G. F. Nuttall, 'Cambridge Nonconformity 1660-1710: From Holcroft to Hussey', *Journal of the United Reformed Church History Society,* I, 241-58.

6   Joseph Hussey, *God's Operations of Grace but no offers of grace,* 1707.

7   R. Tudur Jones, op.cit., 115-16.

8   *A Declaration of the Congregational Ministry in and about London against Antinomian Errors and Ignorant and Scandalous Persons intruding themselves into the Ministry,* 1699, 10.

9   For example Benjamin Keach, *A Golden Mine Opened,* 1694, 69: 'God calls, nay cries to you sinners ... He sends his Ministers to call you, to invite you, who tell you all things are now ready'; see Raymond Brown, 'Baptist Preaching in Early Eighteenth Century England', *B.Q.,* XXI, 13-18.

10 Benjamin Keach, *A Feast of Fat Things Full of Marrow,* 1696, 75 (Hymn 54), :
             Rebels! (saith God) lay down your Arms
             and make your Peace with me;
         O quickly now, come in to-day
             you shall forgiven be!

11 Charles Haddon Spurgeon, *The Metropolitan Tabernacle: its history and work,* 1876, 39.

12 Matthias Maurice, *The Modern Question Modestly Answered,* 1737, 3-4, 22; cf. G. F. Nuttall, 'Northamptonshire and *The Modern Question:* A Turning Point in Eighteenth Century Dissent', *Journal of Theological Studies* XVI, n.s., 101-23.

13 G. F. Nuttall, *Calendar,* Letter 416.

14 John Rippon, *A Brief Memoir of the life and writing of the late Rev. John Gill D.D.,* 1838, 56, 100-104, and John Brine, *The Moral Law the rule of moral conduct to believers,* 1792.

15 John Brine, *A Refutation of Arminian Principles,* 1743, 21.

16 [C. E. Shipley, ed.], *The Baptists of Yorkshire,* 1912, 89-90. For an outline of Jackson's theology and a selection of his hymns, see E. R. Lewis, *History of the Bethesda Baptist Church, Barnoldswick, Yorks,* Cwmavon 1893, 17-64.

17 John Brine, *Motives to Love and Unity among Calvinists,* 1753, 59-60.

18 For Foster see Walter Wilson, op.cit., II, 270-83; Ivimey III, 215, 399-404; Charles Bulkley, *A Sermon preached ... on the occasion of the death of the late Rev. James Foster,* 1753, and Caleb Fleming, *A Sermon preached at Pinners' Hall on the occasion of the death of the Rev. James Foster with memoirs of his life and character,* 1753.

19 C. H. Spurgeon, op.cit., 47.

20 Walter Wilson, op.cit., IV, 218.

21 G. F. Nuttall, *Calendar,* Letter 1428.

22 Jonathan Edwards, *Works of Jonathan Edwards,* Edinburgh 1974, I, 347, 348, 344.

23 Ibid., 344.

24 J. G. Fuller, op.cit., 40.

25 Ibid., 43.

26 Ibid., 44-5.

27 Ibid., 46-7.

28 E. A. Payne, *Baptists of Berkshire,* 1951, 79.

29 Jonathan Edwards, op.cit., 344.

30 E. F. Kevan, op.cit., 80-82; C. B. Jewson, *The Baptists in Norfolk,* 1957, 53; cf. also W. T. Whitley, 'General Baptists in Surrey and Sussex', *B.Q.,* IV. 70.

31 Sermon on 'Free Grace', *Wesley's Works,* 1872, VII, 383.

32 John Telford (ed.), *The Letters of the Rev. John Wesley, A.M.,* 8 vols, 1931, I, 351.

33 George Whitefield, *Journal,* 1960, 583.

34 Nehemiah Curnock (ed.), *The Journal of the Rev. John Wesley, A.M.,* 8 vols, 1938, II, 135; III, 232, 296; V, 180, 195; VII, 132.

35 J. C. Whitebrook, 'The life and works of Mrs Anne Dutton', *T.B.H.S.* VII, 129-46.

36 Ibid., 141-6.

37 G. F. Nuttall, *Howel Harris, the Last Enthusiast,* Cardiff 1965.

38 Frank Baker, *William Grimshaw 1708-63,* 1963, 245. For a good account of Yorkshire Baptist churches which owed their beginnings to the Evangelical Revival see [C. E. Shipley, ed.], op.cit., 98-111.

39 *B.A.R.,* II, 100-108; J. H. J. Plumbridge, 'The Life and Letters of John Parker', *B.Q.,* VIII, 111-22; *Letters to his friends by the Rev. John Parker ... with a sketch of his life and character by John Fawcett,* Leeds 1794. For Crabtree, Hartley and Smith, see Isaac Mann, *Memoirs of the late Rev. William Crabtree,* 1815; *B.A.R.,* III, 393-6.

40 Frank Baker, op.cit., 271; *Letters to his friends ... Fawcett,* op.cit., 11.

41 S. L. Ollard and P. C. Walker (ed.), *Archbishop Herring's Visitation Returns 1743,* Yorkshire Archaeological Society: Record Series LXXI (1928), v - xxiv.

42 Frank Baker, op.cit., 243.

43 L. G. Champion, *Farthing Rushlight: The Story of Andrew Gifford 1700-84,* 1961, 26.

44 Ibid., 5.

45 Ivimey, III, 604; cf. Tom Beynon (ed.), *Howel Harris's Visits to London,* Aberystwyth 1960, 66, 69, 72, 76, 87, 97, 101, 113, 143 for occasions when Harris visited the Gifford home.

46 Ernest A. Payne, 'An Elegy on Andrew Gifford', *B.Q.,* IX, 54-7.

47 [Sarah Medley], *Memoirs of the late Rev. Samuel Medley,* Liverpool, 1833.

48 Graham W. Hughes, *With Freedom Fired,* 1955.

49 Luke Tyerman, *The Life of the Rev. George Whitefield,* 2 vols., 2nd edn, 1890, II, 408; Graham W. Hughes, op.cit., 12.

50 W. T. Whitley, 'The Influence of Whitefield on Baptists', *B.Q.,* V, 30-36.

51   J. Fawcett, Jnr, *An Account of the life, ministry and writings of the late Rev. John Fawcett,* 1818.

52   A. S. Langley, 'Abraham Greenwood 1749-1827', *B.Q.,* II, 84-9.

53   G. P. Gould, *The Baptist College at Regent's Park,* 1910, 14-15.

54   'John Ward LL.D., F.R.S., F.S.A.', *T.B.H.S.,* IV, 1-32; E. J. Tongue, 'Dr John Ward's Trust', *B.Q.,* XIII, 221-7, 267-75.

55   Matthew Poole, *A Model for the maintaining of students ... principally in order to the Ministry,* 1658: in a letter by Richard Baxter, 'To the Rich that love Christ', 9; Richard Baxter, *The Crucifying of the World,* 1658, preface: 'Catalogue of seasonable good works', 7.

56   Joseph Stennett, *The Complaints of an Unsuccessful Ministry,* 1753, vii.

57   Ibid., 16. The Evangelical Revival's emphasis on the religion of the 'heart' being as important as doctrinal orthodoxy often recurs in association letters from the mid-eighteenth century onwards, see, for example, letter of the Midland Association 1766, 2: 'Vain it will be to plead that we have assented to the doctrines of the Gospel unless we *feel* their sanctifying influence in our hearts'; cf. also letters of Western Association, 1771, 2; 1778, 3; Kent and Sussex Association 1781, 4-7; Midland Association 1789, 3-5.

58   James Hargreaves, *The Life and Memoir of the Rev. John Hirst,* Rochdale 1816, 359-60, 374-9; cf. *B.Q.,* VIII, 52; Isaac Mann, op.cit., 31-2.

59   Robert Dawbarn (ed.), *History of a Forgotten Sect of Baptised Believers,* n.d.; *T.B.H.S.,* III, 54-61; Edward Deacon, *Samuel Fisher, Baptist Minister,* Bridgeport, U.S.A., 1911.

60   John Johnson, *The Faith of God's Elect,* Liverpool 1754.

61   John Brine, *Some Mistakes in a book of Mr Johnson's of Liverpool noted and rectified,* 1755.

62   *A Manual of Church Discipline especially designed for the congregation in the Upper Hill Street Chapel, Wisbech, and their connections in other parts,* 1861, 36.

63   A. G. Fuller (ed.), op.cit., xxiv.

64   J. Stennett, *Complaints ... Ministry,* 36.

65   W. T. Whitley, 'Yorkshire and Lancashire Association Minutes, June 1764', *B.Q.,* VIII, 52-80.

66   T. S. H. Elwyn, *The Northamptonshire Baptist Association: a short history,* 1964, 13.

67   *The Circular Letter from the Ministers and Messengers assembled at Kettering, May 22-23, 1770,* 8. For Martin see [John Martin], *Some Account of the Life and Writings of the Rev. John Martin,* 1797.

68   Robert Hall, Snr, *Helps to Zion's Travellers,* Bristol 1781, 117-18.

69   See *T.B.H.S.,* III, 83.

70   W. T. Owen, *Edward Williams,* Cardiff 1963.

71   W. R. Ward, *Religion and Society in England 1790-1850,* 1972, 73.

72   Anne Steele, *Hymns, Psalms and Poems,* 1882, 100, 37.

73   *A Letter to the Rev. Mr John Gill ... by a lover of the truth,* 1737, 6-7.

74   Olinthus Gregory (ed.), op.cit., VI ('Conversational Remarks'), 125.

75   John Julian (ed.), *A Dictionary of Hymnology,* 1915, 112, cf. 148; Hugh Martin (ed.), *The Baptist Hymn Book Companion,* 1962, 261, and *History of the Baptist Church at Wainsgate, Hebden Bridge 1750-1950,* n.d., 8.

76   G. F. Nuttall, 'Letters by Benjamin Francis', 7.

77   Walter Wilson, op.cit., IV, 227.

78   William Button, *Remarks on The Gospel worthy of all acceptation,* 1785, and Andrew Fuller, *A Defence of a Treatise entitled The Gospel worthy of all acceptation,* 1787.

79   Robert Hall, Snr, op.cit., 118. For an exposition of Fullerism, see E. F. Clipsham, 'Andrew Fuller and Fullerism: a study of Evangelical Calvinism', *B.Q.,* XX, 99-114, 146-54, 214-25, 268-76.

Chapter 6 : The parting of the ways

1   *M.G.A.,* II, 159.

2   Wood, 177-8.

3   Ibid., 179-80.

4   *M.G.A.,* II, 188-9 note.

5   Ibid., 256-7.

6   Ibid., 188.

7   Ibid., 179-256.

8   Ibid., 154, 160, 196.

9   Ibid., 147.

10 Ibid., 230.

11 Ibid., 171, 238.

12 Ibid., 190, 233.

13 Ibid., 190.

14 Ibid., 209.

15 Ibid., 214-15; cf. [W. T. Whitley], 'The General Baptist Academy of the Old Connexion', *B.Q.,* III, 331.

16 For John Evans see *D.N.B., Dictionary of Welsh Biography.*

17 *B.Q.,* III, 331-2.

18 John Evans, *A Brief Sketch of the Several Denominations,* (ed. James Aikman), Edinburgh 1839, vi.

19 *M.G.A.,* II, 221; cf. C. B. Jewson, op.cit., 61.

20 *M.G.A.,* I, 125, 141, 146; II, 41, 48, 54, 214 note, et passim.

21 *B.A.R.,* I, 117.

22 Ibid., 100.

23 *M.G.A.,* II, 227.

24 Ibid., 307-10.

25 Ibid., 169.

26 Roy Porter, op.cit., 255; James Woodforde (ed. John Beresford), *The Diary of a Country Parson 1758-1802,*

Oxford 1978, 99, 107, 115, 150, et passim.

27 Roy Porter, op.cit., 256.

28 *M.G.A.*, II, 194.

29 E. Douglas Bebb, *Wesley: A Man with a Concern,* 1950, 69; cf. Thomas Blanshard, *The Life of Samuel Bradburn,* 1871, 146: many of the Methodist people came to regard it as 'a drug composed of the *slave dealer's sin* and *the slaves' misery';* see also Samuel Bradburn, *An Address to the People called Methodists concerning the evil of encouraging the slave trade,* Manchester 1792, 12, 18-24; Thomas Clarkson, *The History of the Rise, Progress and Accomplishment of the Abolition of the Slave Trade,* 2 vols., 1808, II, 347-50. Carey made the suggestion that money thus saved might be given to overseas missions, William Carey, *An Enquiry into the obligation of Christians to use means for the conversion of the heathens,* Leicester 1792, 86.

30 Roy Porter, op.cit., 151-2.

31 Ibid., 216-17, 219.

32 *M.G.A.*, II, 197.

33 Ibid., 292.

34 Ibid., 141.

35 Ibid., 159.

36 Wood, 177-8.

37 Ernest A. Payne, 'The Venerable John Stanger of Bessels Green', *B.Q.*, XXVII, 300-20.

38 Ibid., 314-5. From 1770 onwards it was not unusual for some disillusioned General Baptist members to leave their churches in order to join a local Particular Baptist church, newly revived by moderate Calvinism, e.g. the sixteen members who 'ran away' from Chesham to New Mill, 'a Particular Baptist or rather a Methodist society' (L. G. Champion (ed.), *Berkhamsted, Chesham and Tring,* 153-4). The Particular Baptists at New Mill had come under the influence of the Evangelical Revival 'as the result of work by some of George Whitefield's associates' as well as one of his converts, Samuel Medley, minister at Watford, cf. D. R. Watts, *A History of the Hertfordshire Baptists,* Hertfordshire Baptist Association 1978, 15.

39 *M.G.A.*, II, 179-80, 182-4.

40 Wood, 188.

41 *M.G.A.*, II, 186.

42 Ibid., 213 note.

43 William Vidler, *A Sketch of the life of Elhanan Winchester, preacher of the Universal Restoration,* 1797, and *A Testimony of Respect to the memory of Elhanan Winchester* 1797; see also Adam Taylor, *Memoirs ... Dan Taylor,* 188-192, 262-66.

44 *B.Q.*, XXVII, 315.

45 Frank Buffard, op.cit., 53; F. W. Butt-Thompson, 'William Vidler', *B.Q.*, XVII, 3-9.

46 *B.A.R.*, II, 33.

47 Alexander Gordon, *Addresses Biographical and Historical,* 1922, 313-29, and Stuart Mews, 'Reason and Emotion in Working-Class Religion' in Derek Baker (ed.), *Schism, Heresy and Religious Protest,* Studies in Church History, IX, Cambridge 1972, 365-82.

48 *M.G.A.*, II, 244.

49 Ibid., 245.

50 Ibid., 256-7.

51 R. B. Aspland, *Memoir of the life, works and correspondence of the Rev. Robert Aspland of Hackney,* 1850.

52 *M.G.A.*, II, 271.

53 Ibid., 277.

54 Ibid., 276.

55 *General Baptist Repository,* V, No. XXVIII, 183.

56 *The Monthly Repository of Theology and General Literature,* X (1815), 320.

57 'A Sussex Lay Preacher seeing Camp Meetings in America', *B.Q.*, IV, 324-5.

58 Wood, 218-20.

59 Ibid., 196.

60 Taylor, II, 327.

61 Adam Taylor, *Memoirs ... Dan Taylor,* 324-6.

62   Op.cit., 221; Wood, 197.

63   Taylor II, 456.

64   Wood, 219, 302-4; Taylor II, 455-6.

65   Wood, 197.

66   S. C. Osborne, *The First Two Hundred Years* (Hinckley Baptist church), Hinckley 1966; for the town's late eighteenth century social conditions see H. J. Francis, *A History of Hinckley,* Hinckley 1930, 127-29.

67   Taylor II, 356-7.

68   Ibid., 468-9.

69   Ibid., 394-6.

70   Wood, 186-7.

71   Ibid., 195.

72   Taylor II, 375.

73   S. C. Osborne, op.cit., 33.

74   G. P. R. Prosser, 'The Formation of the General Baptist Missionary Society', *B.Q.,* XXII, 23-29.

Chapter 7 : 'A glorious door'

1   Caleb Evans, *A Charge and Sermon; delivered at the ordination of Thomas Dunscombe,* Bristol 1773, 6.

2   K. R. Manley, 'The Making of an Evangelical Baptist Leader', *B.Q.,* XXVI, 268.

3   *B.A.R.,* II, 459-64.

4   Caleb Evans, *The Kingdom of God,* Bristol [1775], 24.

5   Robert Hall, Snr,op.cit., 117.

6   George Smith, *The Life of William Carey,* 1909, 12.

7   Kenneth W. H. Howard, 'John Sutcliff of Olney', *B.Q.,* XIV, 304-9; A. G. Fuller, op.cit., 637-44, 'The Principles and Prospects of a Servant of Christ'.

8   *The Nature, Evidences and Advantages of Humility presented in a Circular Letter ... the Baptist Association assembled at Nottingham, June 2-3, 1784,* 12; cf. T. S. H. Elwyn, op.cit., 16-17; Ernest A. Payne, *The Prayer Call of 1784,* 1941.

9   News of eight-hundred conversions in New England brought inspiration to the Western Association in 1781, cf. *The Elders and Messengers of Several Baptist Churches meeting at Pithay, Bristol, 1781,* 2; J. G. Fuller, op.cit., 53.

10 For example, *The Kent and Sussex Association of Baptist Churches ... assembled at Brighthelmston, 5-6 June 1792,* 4; but note that several years before Sutcliff's 'Prayer Call', the Midland Association made the request that its churches devote every Friday evening to prayer 'for the revival of God's work', (*The Circular Letter of the Elders and Messengers ... maintaining the great doctrines ... final perseverance... 1767,* 8.

11 John Ryland, *The Work of Faith ... illustrated in the life and death of the Rev. Andrew Fuller,* 1816, 153 note; the 'Prayer Call' had not restricted its invitation to the Particular Baptists, cf. *The Nature, Evidences,* op.cit., 12: 'We shall rejoice if any other Christian society of our own or other denominations will unite with us, and do now invite them most cordially to join heart and hand in the attempt'.

12 George Burder, *United Prayer for the Spread of the Gospel earnestly recommended, or an Abridgement of An Humble Attempt...,* 1814, 4.

13 Ernest A. Payne, *The Growth of the World Church,* 1955.

14 K. R. Manley, op.cit., 254-74, 'John Rippon and Baptist Historiography', *B.Q.,* XXVIII, 109-25.

15 Before the appearance of Rippon's *Register,* association printed letters frequently conveyed the message of moderate Calvinism to the churches, e.g. letters of the Western Association 1775, 6; 1778, 2-3; Kent and Sussex Association 1784, 7; Yorkshire and Lancashire Association 1787, 8.

16 *B.A.R.,* I, 167.

17 Ibid., 247-56.

18 S. Pearce Carey, *William Carey,* 1923.

19 *B.A.R.,* I, 322.

20 S. Pearce Carey, *Samuel Pearce, M.A.: The Baptist Brainerd,* n.d., 139. For Pearce see also Andrew Fuller's 'Memoirs of Samuel Pearce' in A. G. Fuller,

op.cit., 760-95; Ernest A. Payne, 'Some Sidelights on Pearce and his friends', *B.Q.,* VII, 270-75, 'Some Samuel Pearce Documents', *B.Q.,* XVIII, 126-34.

21 Gilbert Laws, *Andrew Fuller,* 1942, 62, 63, 66, 71. For the relatively poor initial support of London ministers see C. B. Lewis, *The Life of John Thomas,* 1873, 226-27.

22 *B.A.R.,* I, 418; J. G. Fuller, op.cit., 55-6. In 1791 the churches of the Yorkshire and Lancashire Association described the slave trade as 'the most horrid and diabolical practice that ever disgraced the conduct of mankind', cf. *The Dissenting Ministers of the Baptist Denomination in Association at Salendine Nook, June 15-16, 1791,* 5.

23 Richard Baxter, *A Christian Directory* ..., 1673, 559.

24 For cruelties reported at Bristol and Liverpool, see Thomas Clarkson, op.cit., I, 292-367, 371-44; cf. Dorothy Marshall, *Eighteenth Century England,* 1962, 244 for Liverpool's increasing dominance over Bristol in the trade. For Caleb Evans' and John Ryland's support for the abolitionist cause in Bristol, see W. M. S. West, 'Methodists and Baptists in Eighteenth Century Bristol', *Proceedings of the Wesley Historical Society,* XLIV, 166.

25 W. T. Whitley, 'The Tune Book of 1791', *B.Q.,* X, 438-42; N. S. Moon, op.cit., 35; Basil Amey, 'Baptist Missionary Society Radicals', *B.Q.,* XXVI, 363-376; and K. R. M. Short, 'A Note on the Sierra Leone Mission and Religious Freedom, 1796', *B.Q.,* XXVIII, 355-60.

26 *B.A.R.,* I, 418-19.

27 [W. T. Whitley], 'A Calendar of Letters', *B.Q.,* VI, 220-1.

28 G. F. Nuttall, 'Questions and Answers: an eighteenth century correspondence', *B.Q.,* XXVII, 89.

29 Ivimey, IV, 453-4.

30 For Baptist itinerancy in this period see Deryck W. Lovegrove, 'Particular Baptist Itinerant Preachers during the late 18th and early 19th Centuries', *B.Q.,* XXVIII, 127-41; Charles Brown, *The Story of Baptist Home Missions,* 1897.

31 Ivimey, IV, 364-79; E. F. Kevan, op.cit., 117-35; and

Ernest A. Payne, 'Abraham Booth 1734-1806', *B.Q.,* XXVI, 28-42.

32 D. W. Lovegrove, op.cit., 129-30; Frank Buffard, op.cit., 54. Ministers who engaged in evangelistic preaching were sometimes criticised by high Calvinist members, see John Howard Hinton, *A Biographical Portraiture of the late Rev. James Hinton,* 1824, 149, 266-7, and also Lawrence Butterworth's experience at Evesham in 1785 where, despite a building 'crowded with attentive hearers of the word ... there were several members of the society that did not approve of the measure of bringing the gospel into Evesham' ('Lawrence Butterworth's Book' at Evesham Baptist Church, f.9).

33 G. F. Nuttall, 'Questions and Answers', 89.

34 For the Society's evangelistic, educational and social work in Ireland see J. Belcher and A. G. Fuller, *The Baptist Irish Society,* 1845, Ernest A. Payne, *The Baptist Union: A Short History,* 1959, 46-7, D. P. Kingdon, *Baptist Evangelism in 19th Century Ireland,* Belfast 1965, George Pritchard, *Memoirs of the life and writings of the Rev. Joseph Ivimey,* 1835, 86-105.

35 *B.A.R.,* II, 447; S. P. Carey, *Samuel Pearce,* 83.

36 D. W. Lovegrove, op.cit., 130-31; M. F. Hewitt, 'Sutcliff's Academy at Olney', *B.Q.,* IV, 276-9.

37 Cambridge (St Andrew's Street) Church Book, May 14, 1775, f.83.

38 Ms. FPC E.16 (31), Rippon Collection in Angus Library, Regent's Park College, Oxford, in a long letter (20 May 1795) from Joshua Thomas in answer to Rippon's question 'What endeavours have the Baptists made for a learned ministry since the Reformation?'

39 George Dyer, *Memoirs of the life and writings of Robert Robinson,* 1796, 186-92, 468-71, and G. W. Hughes, op.cit., 92-3.

40 N. S. Moon, op.cit., 11.

41 N. S. Moon, 'Caleb Evans, Founder of the Bristol Education Society', *B.Q.,* XXIV, 175-90.

42 N. S. Moon, *Education for Ministry,* 129-31, Appendix A 'The Case for an Educated Ministry: Bristol Education Society 1770'.

43   G. P. Gould, op.cit., 14-16.

44   Ibid., 16-19.

45   George Pritchard, *Memoirs of the Rev. William Newman,* 1837.

46   G. P. Gould, op.cit., 20-49; R. E. Cooper, *From Stepney to St Giles,* 1960; and Ernest A. Payne (ed.), *Studies in History and Religion presented to Dr H. Wheeler Robinson,* 1942, 229-37.

47   Thomas Steadman, *Memoir of the Rev. William Steadman D.D.,* 1838, 227-28. For the formation of the Northern Education Society and its invitation to Steadman, see ibid., 212-24; cf. also John O. Barrett, *A Short History of Rawdon College,* 1954.

48   [C. E. Shipley, ed.], op.cit., 286; cf. A. C. Underwood, 'The Early Relations of Horton Academy and Rawdon College with Lancashire', *B.Q.,* V, 130-36; C. B. Whyatt, 'The Distressed State of the Country ...', *B.Q.,* XII, 208-20.

49   [C. E. Shipley, ed.] op.cit., 827.

50   John Gadsby, *A Memoir of the late Mr William Gadsby,* 1844.

51   Ibid., 61; cf. W. R. Ward, op.cit., 73 and. on the role of associations in this context, see *The Utility of Associations: a Circular Letter addressed to the Baptist Churches ... met in association at Rochdale* (Yorkshire and Lancashire Association), Bradford, 1807.

52   Ibid., 32-6.

53   A. J. Klaiber, *The Story of the Suffolk Baptists,* 1939, 49, 112.

54   John Browne, *The History of Congregationalism ... in Norfolk and Suffolk,* 1877, 566.

55   A. J. Klaiber, op.cit., 117; see also Kenneth Dix, 'Particular Baptists and Strict Baptists: An Historical Survey', *Strict Baptist Historical Society Bulletin,* No.13 (1976).

56   Ernest A. Payne, *The Fellowship of Believers,* 1962, 65, 80, 'Abraham Atkins and General Communion', *B.Q.,* XXVI, 314-19; R. W. Oliver, 'John Collett Ryland, Daniel Turner and the Communion Controversy 1772-1781', *B.Q.,* XXIX, 77-79, and C. B. Jewson, 'St

Mary's, Norwich', *B.Q.*, X, 340-46.

57 For the use of printed Association Letters to encourage Baptists in other parts of the country, see the Western Association reports of increased membership figures supplied by other associations, e.g. *The Elders and Messengers ... met at Horsley, June 10-11, 1778*, 8.

58 E. A. Payne, *Baptist Union*, 1958, 19-21.

59 For clerical and lay opposition to Baptist itinerancy see John Howard Hinton, op.cit., 257-9, and Thomas Steadman, op.cit., 160, 173.

60 See *The Circular Letter of the Eastern Association held at Hemel Hempstead, Herts, May 14-15, 1776*, 10 for Robert Robinson's assertion of the Baptist people's loyalty to their country: 'There is nothing in our principles destructive of the peace of civil society; nothing hostile to government'.

61 Ernest A. Payne, 'Nonconformists and the American Revolution', *Journal of the United Reformed Church History Society*, I, 210-27, and W. M. S. West, op.cit., 161-66.

62 Letter to Thomas Cushing, July 7, 1773 in W. T. Franklin, *Memoirs of the life and writings of Benjamin Franklin*, 3 vols, 1818, II, 191.

63 W[arren], R. H., *The Hall Family*, Bristol, 1910,12. Several association letters make reference to 'the unhappy contest with America', cf. *The Circular Letter ... of the several Baptist Churches ... met in Association at Birmingham, May 20-21, 1777*, 6; see also Western Association Letters, 1775, 1; 1776, 3; 1780, 3.

64 Quoted in W. T. Whitley, *Baptist Bibliography*, 2 vols, 1916, I, 201, and see Thomas Steadman, op.cit., 11 for the young Steadman's support for 'the independence of the Americans'; for the interaction between these events and nonconformist politics, see James E. Bradley, 'Religion and Reform at the Polls: Nonconformity in Cambridge Politics, 1774-1784', *Journal of British Studies*, XXIII (2), 1984, 55-78.

65 Eastern Association Book 1775-80, 42, in Angus Library, Regent's Park College, Oxford.

66 *The Parliamentary History of England*, XXVI (1786-88), 27 GEORGE III, 1816, 831.

67   Ibid., XXVIII (1789-91), 30 GEORGE III, 1816, 436.

68   For attacks on dissenters' homes and meeting-houses at the time of the French Revolution, see S. P. Carey, *Samuel Pearce,* 28-32, J. H. Hinton, op.cit., 255-65. These fears continued, sometimes inflamed by nonconformist preaching; note the embarrassment of the Baptist Board concerning a sermon-lecture preached by John Martin in 1798, the year following the Spithead naval mutinies and the attempted invasion on the Pembrokeshire coast by the French fleet. Martin, it was reported, said that in the event of a successful French landing 'many of the Dissenters, both Baptists and Paedobaptists, would join them', a sentiment vigorously opposed by the Board who dismissed him from membership, cf. E. A. Payne, 'Abraham Booth', 39-40; *T.B.H.S.,* VI, 92-94.

69   *Parliamentary History of England,* XXVIII (1789-91) 30 GEORGE III, 1816, 436-7.

70   Richard Price, *A Discourse on the Love of our Country,* 1789, 50.

71   Robert Hall, Jnr, *Christianity consistent with a love of freedom,* in *Works* III, 10, 15, 21-2.

72   C. B. Jewson, 'Norwich Baptists and the French Revolution', B.Q., XXIV, 212. For Norwich radicalism in this period, see C. B. Jewson, *Jacobin City: A Portrait of Norwich in its reaction to the French Revolution 1788-1802,* Glasgow, 1975.

73   C. B. Jewson, 'Norwich Baptists ... French Revolution', 215; see also Deryck Lovegrove, 'English Evangelical Dissent and the European Conflict 1789-1815' in W. J. Sheils (ed.), *The Church and War,* Studies in Church History, XX, 1983, 263-276.

74   William Carey, op.cit., 79.

75   *Parliamentary Debates* (First Series) XIX, cols.128-33, quoted in D. M. Thompson, *Nonconformity in the Nineteenth Century,* 1972, 29-31.

76   Douglas C. Sparkes, 'The Test Act of 1673 and its aftermath', B.Q., XXV, 74-85; cf. T. W. Davis (ed.), *Committees for the Repeal of the Test and Corporation Acts: Minutes 1786-90 and 1827-8,* (London Record Society XIV), 1978.

77   Maldwyn Edwards, *After Wesley: a study of the social and political influence of Methodism in the middle period (1791-1849),* 1935, 75-82. Bernard L. Manning,

op.cit., 130-43. W. R. Ward, op.cit., 56, points out that at this time John Wilks formed 'a mixed movement of evangelical dissenters and Methodists, which as the Protestant Society became his permanent star vehicle'.

78   Gwynne Lewis, 'British Nonconformist-reactions to the persecution of Protestants in France, 1815-1819', *Proceedings of the Huguenot Society of London* XX:5, 510-27; see also *Evangelical Magazine,* 1815, 421-2, 543-4, 553; 1816, 31-2, 97, 107-9; *Baptist Magazine* 1815, 478-80, 518, 528.

79   Thomas Clarkson, op.cit., I, 366.

80   John Leifchild, *Memoir of the late Rev. Joseph Hughes,* 1835, 172; for Hughes see also F. H. Gale, *Battersea Chapel 1797-1897,* 1897, 14-38.

81   Thomas Steadman, op.cit., 146, 157-60, 162, 164, 166, 186.

82   Ibid., 157, 186-7.

83   T. W. Laqueuer, *Religion and Respectability: Sunday Schools and Working Class Culture 1780-1850,* Yale, New Haven, 1976, 2.

84   Revolutionary fears were behind the fierce criticism expressed both in the House of Lords and in print by the Bishop of Rochester, Samuel Horsley. In one of the most strident sermons against some aspects of the new movement he described a number of them as 'Schools of Jacobinical Religion ... Religion in the shape and disguise of Charity Schools and Sunday Schools'. His published Charge of 1800 was one reason why many Anglicans withdrew support from inter-denominational Sunday Schools at the turn of the century, cf. *The Charge of Samuel, Lord Bishop of Rochester to the Clergy of his Diocese...,* 1800, 25-6. For Robert Hall, Jnr's comments on Horsley's *Charge* see his *Defence of Village Preaching* in Olinthus Gregory (ed.), op.cit., III, 329-384.

85   Joseph Ivimey, *Memoir of William Fox Esq.,* 1831, cf. William Morton Pitt, *Plan for the Extension and Regulation of Sunday Schools,* 1786, a popular manual published by the Sunday School Society only six months after its formation.

86   T. W. Laqueuer, op.cit., 63.

87   John Wesley, *Journal,* VII, 3. For a description of the work of a smaller rural Sunday School at Horsley,

Glos., at this time see G. F. Nuttall, 'Letters by Benjamin Francis', 7.

88 J. W. Morris, *A Discouse delivered at Clipston, March 11, 1792 ... in favour of Sunday Schools,* Market Harborough, 1792, 9.

89 Daniel Turner, *Hints on Religious Education, being two sermons in favour of Sunday Schools,* 1794, 9-10; cf. John Liddon, *The General Religious Instruction of the Poor, the surest means of providing national happiness: a sermon on Sunday Schools,* 1792, 16: 'a well instructed Christian peasantry will constitute the support and happiness of the nation'.

90 James Dore, *A Sermon preached at Maze Pond, Southwark, Sept. 27, 1789 for the benefit of the Society established in London ...,* 1789, 12, 32; cf. Robert Hall, Jnr, *The Advantages of knowledge to the lower classes: ... for the benefit of a Sunday School* in Olinthus Gregory, op.cit., I, 193-218.

91 For the Religious Tract society and other pan-evangelical organisations in this period, cf. Roger H. Martin, *Evangelicals United: Ecumenical Stirrings in Pre-Victorian Britain, 1795-1830,* Metuchen, New Jersey, 1983.

92 William Canton, *A History of the British and Foreign Bible Society,* 5 vols, 1904-10, I, 9-10.

93 John Leifchild, op.cit., 166; for the Clapham Sect see Ernest Marshall Howse, *Saints in Politics,* 1953 and Sir James Stephen, *Essays in Ecclesiastical Biography,* 2 vols, 1849.

94 John Leifchild, op.cit., 219.

95 *B.Q.,* XVIII, 30.

96 Roger H. Martin, op.cit., 178.

97 William Carey, op.cit., 84.

98 Letter from William Carey to Andrew Fuller, Calcutta, May 15, 1806, quoted in E. Daniel Potts, *British Baptist Missionaries in India 1793-1837,* Cambridge 1967, 53. For Baptist missionaries' relationship with other Christians in India during this period, see ibid., 49-61.

99 S. P. Carey, *Samuel Pearce,* 179.

100 Ibid., 127, 179, 162.

101 Ibid., 145; Gilbert Laws, op.cit., 94-5.

102 Berridge's itinerant ministry in Cambridgeshire issued directly in the 'formation of Baptist churches in Waterbeach, Stretham, Swavesey, Bottisham Lode, Haddenham and Harston. For Berridge see Richard Whittingham, *The Works of the Rev. John Berridge ... with an enlarged memoir of his Life,* 1838, and Charles Smyth, *Simeon and Church Order,* Cambridge 1940, 149-200. It was Simeon who said of itinerants like Berridge, 'the clergyman beats the bush, and the Dissenters catch the game' (William Carus, *Memoirs of the Life of the Rev. Charles Simeon,* 1847, 139).

103 Rippon's popular hymn books included hymns by Doddridge, Cowper, Newton, Cruttenden, Toplady as well as Isaac Watts and those by Baptist authors.

104 For an example of books written by non-Baptists and appreciatively read by a young Baptist theological student in the late eighteenth century, see W. Yates, *Memoirs of Mr John Chamberlain,* Calcutta 1824. These include works by Cotton Mather, Baxter, Philip and Matthew Henry, Thomas Halyburton, Jonathan Edwards, David Brainerd, John Eliot, John Gillies. Evangelical Anglicans also expressed warm appreciation of Baptist authors, e.g. Henry Venn's commendation of Booth's *Reign of Grace, (B.Q.,* XXVI, 31) and Richard Cecil's praise of Fuller's *Gospel Worthy ...* (Gilbert Laws, op.cit., 94-5).

105 Notes of a Church Meeting held at Whitchurch, Hampshire, 18 October 1789, Angus Library, Regent's Park College, Oxford.

106 *The Circular Letter ... Association at Cirencester, May 25-6, 1779,* 10.

107 *The Dissenting Ministers of the Baptist Denomination in Association at Salendine Nook June 15-16, 1791,* 7-8.

108 Samuel Greatheed, *General Union Recommended to Real Christians,* 1798.

109 Some dissenters were not remotely happy about the new pan-evangelical societies and deplored the 'laxity of principle' involved in post-Evangelical Revival ecumenism; see David M. Thompson, *Denominationalism and Dissent, 1795-1835: a question of identity,* Friends of Dr Williams's Library Lecture 1985, for the view that 'the new denominationalism was the result of the Revival and not a reaction against it'.

110 Thomas Steadman, op.cit., 167-8.

111 Ibid., 187; for Chamberlain see W. Yates, op.cit., C. B. Lewis, *John Chamberlain: a Missionary Biography,* Calcutta 1876, and Ernest A. Payne, *The First Generation,* 1936.

* * * * * * * * *

INDEX

ABBE, T. and HOWSON, H.E. 147

ABERDEEN 84,100,108

ABINGDON 78,130

ACADEMIES
General refs 2,51,53,91,131, 144,152
Bristol 49,72,82,83,84,93,94, 100,108,115,117, 118,119, 120,121,122,124,125-7,128, 136,151,154
Horton (Northern) 127,128, 129,167
Mile End (New Connexion) 100,110
Newington Green 2
Olney (Sutcliff's) 82,124, 126,166
Ponders End, later Islington (General Baptist) 100,160
Rawdon 167
Stepney 127,138,158,167
Wainsgate (Fawcett's), later at Branday Hall 82,83, 124,126

ADAMS, Richard 25,50

AFRICA 102,117,118,121,122

AIKMAN, James 160

ALLEN, Richard 25,26,54, 152

AMERICA
General refs 31,109,117,118, 122,162
Baptists of 31,46,101
Declaration of Independence 135
War of Independence 132, 133,168

AMERSHAM, Bucks 148

AMEY, Basil 165

AMSTERDAM 32

ANABAPTISM 21,29,79,149

ANGLICANS 1,2,7,9,36,52, 53,79,80,82,127,132,133, 136,137,138,139,140,170,172

ANNE, Queen 2,3,6,53

ANOINTING OF THE SICK 18

ANTINOMIANISM 5,9,74,155

ARIANISM 27,41,133,150

ARMINIANISM 26,27,34,40,66, 68,71,74,75,78,79,82,86,98, 103,126,129,146,155

ARNESBY, Leics 89,115,116, 134

ASH, John 84,93

ASHTON-UNDER-LYNE 112

ASPLAND, R.B. 162

ASPLAND, Robert 108,109, 162

ASSOCIATIONS
General refs 10,35,40,60,63, 84,85-90,91-2,111-12,115, 117,118,129,131,132
General Baptist
Aylesbury 23
Lincolnshire 64,69,98,105
Western 22
Yorkshire 112
Particular Baptist
Abingdon 40
Berkshire 40,150,156
Eastern 133,168
Kent and Sussex 107,154, 158,164
London (1704-6) 8,40-41, 71
Midland 40,140,158,164,168, 172
Norfolk and Suffolk 129
Northamptonshire 83,89,90, 116,120,121,122,123,159, 163
Northern 40
Western 39,40,71,77,78,85, 86,121,123,145,154,158, 164,168
Yorkshire & Lancashire 40,81,85-9,127,128,129, 140,156,157,159,164,165, 167,172

175

185